CHURCH WITHOUT BORDERS

GROWING A MULTIETHNIC COMMUNITY

 A catalogue record for this book is available from the National Library of Australia

CHURCH WITHOUT BORDERS

GROWING A MULTIETHNIC COMMUNITY

MATHEW KURUVILLA

CHURCH WITHOUT BORDERS
Growing a Multiethnic Community

© Mathew Kuruvilla 2019

First published in Australia in 2019

Morling Press
122 Herring Rd
Macquarie Park NSW 2113 Australia
Phone: +61 2 9878 0201
Email: enquiries@morling.edu.au
www.morlingcollege.com/morlingpress

The publication is copyright. Other than for the purposes of study and subject to the conditions of the Copyright Act, no part of this book in any form or by any means (electronic, mechanical, micro-copying, photocopying or otherwise) may be reproduced, stored in a retrieval system, communicated or transmitted without prior written permission.

All Scripture quotations, unless otherwise indicated, are taken from the Holy Bible, New International Version® Anglicised (NIVUK), NIV®. Copyright ©1979, 1984, 2011 by Biblica, Inc.™ Used by permission. All rights reserved worldwide.

ISBN: 978-0-9945726-2-2 (paperback)
ISBN: 978-0-9945726-3-9 (e-book)

Typesetting by Brugel Creative www.brugel.com.au
Cover design by Jason Kuruvilla

CONTENTS

Commendations vii
Foreword xi

Church without Borders

Introduction 3
1. One Asylum Seeker Among the Many 13
Questions for Discussion 25

Part 1: Understanding the Asylum

2. Jesus the Asylum Seeker 29
3. God's Vision for the Asylum 51
4. The Early Church Asylum 64
5. The Future Asylum 79
Questions for Discussion 93

Part 2: Visioning the Asylum

6. The Australian Asylum 97
7. Parkside Church 113
Questions for Discussion 127

Part 3: Gathering the Asylum

8. Building a Multiethnic Asylum 130
9. Nurturing the Asylum 159
10. Leading the Asylum............................ 185
Questions for Discussion 214

Appendices

1. The Homogenous Unit Principle 217
2. Barriers to Multiethnic Ministry 227
3. Language Barriers and Multiple Services........... 234
4. Food Sacrificed to Idols 240
5. The Old Organ or African Style? 243
6. Back to Antioch 249
7. Send the Others to KFC......................... 254
8. The Role of Women 259

Endnotes

Endnotes 269
Acknowledgments 287
About the Author 289

COMMENDATIONS

❝ Mathew Kuruvilla calls on the church and its leaders to break down old barriers and to live faithfully by returning to our Christian multiethnic roots. Through personal stories, his own rich experience at Parkside Church and examination of biblical text, he leads the way in how to build and nurture a true community of diversity.

Rev. Tim Costello AO
Chief Advocate, World Vision Australia

❝ Mathew Kuruvilla has given an important and necessary voice to the biblical injunction for our gospel communities to be ethnically inclusive in Christ. This is a well written and well thought out 'how' and 'why' of the multiethnic church. It is written with conviction and a long history of pastoral experience. I personally know that Mathew's church reflects what he has taught. If the church fails to heed this word, the world will one day wake up and rightly accuse us Christians for claiming a unity in Christ while retreating to segregated enclaves. This is truly a gospel issue.

Ray Galea
Lead Pastor at Multicultural Bible Ministry, Sydney, Australia

---

❝ Mathew Kuruvilla inspires and challenges every Christian to epitomise Jesus by welcoming people of all nations into safe asylums, especially the church. A brilliant, practical 'travel guide' for pastors and leaders on the journey towards creating a place of God's refuge for their multiethnic communities.

Katharine Dale
Multicultural Engagement Officer, The Salvation Army

COMMENDATIONS

❝ Mathew Kuruvilla has proved himself a thought-leading pioneer in the global, growing movement to establish healthy multiethnic churches for the sake of the gospel ... churches in which diverse men and women walk, work and worship God together as one to proclaim a credible witness of God's love for all people. In *Church without Borders*, Mathew shares experiential knowledge gleaned from nearly thirty years of personal and vocational engagement at Parkside Church: insight and wisdom those intending to walk a similar path would do well to internalise, and from which they will greatly benefit.

Dr Mark DeYmaz
Founding Pastor, Mosaic Church of Central Arkansas; co-founder, Mosaix Global Network; author, *Building a Healthy Multiethnic Church* and *Disruption: Repurposing Your Church to Redeem the Community*

❝ Inspired by faithfulness to the Bible and informed by years of church leadership, Mathew Kuruvilla has written a powerful and practical book. He calls us to be the multiethnic body of Christ and in so doing challenges how we do church today. This book comes from the heart and maps out the way forward for multiethnic church discipleship. An essential read!

Rev. Dr Ross Clifford
Principal, Morling College

❝ There is a general anxiety in Australia about refugees, especially those who arrive here by boat. But Mathew Kuruvilla provocatively reframes the whole discussion by casting us all as asylum seekers and the church as the place of true asylum. Therefore, he argues, the church should become a safe harbour for all, a multiethnic community of welcome, hospitality and grace. *Church without Borders* is both inspiring and practical, written by a pastor whose church practises what he's preaching.

Rev. Dr Michael Frost
Morling College, author, *Surprise the World* and *Keep Christianity Weird*

FOREWORD

The assembled congregation described by John in Revelation 7:9–10 is a promise for the globally scattered body of Christ. It is the promise of a church gathered by the Spirit from the four corners of the world without the inconveniences or obstacles imposed by borders or walls.

The modern nation state frequently reinforces these differences of ethnicity, culture and language. More often than not, it makes a virtue of the difference. Indeed, these are the differences that are patrolled, protected, policed and preserved at all costs.

Policies that pursue these ends may reflect the tide of history, but they fly in the face of the future – assuming the apocalyptic visions of John tell us anything about the plans that God has for redeemed humanity. Indeed, John's vision threatens the legitimacy of the assumptions upon which the nations of the world are established: namely, that ethnic and linguistic differences will remain enduring problems for humanity. This premise sees the differences as something to be isolated, solved, avoided or suppressed.

John's vision is otherwise and, for that reason, some evangelicals argue that it is simply a vision for another world. Mathew Kuruvilla would disagree with such a reading of Scripture, and I think he is right to resist such interpretations. Contrary to such a view, the congregation in Revelation 7 witnesses to *one* truth, and it is precisely the *unity* of their praise that is the evidence that God offers salvation to all people, that his throne is raised above all kingdoms of the world, and that his eternal consolation extends from age to age and from nation to nation. Every tribe, people, nation and language acclaim the saving purposes of God towards all people, irrespective of ethnic, cultural or linguistic difference. In short, John describes a church without borders, a church without walls.

This vision has captivated Mathew Kuruvilla's pastoral leadership for three decades in the outer suburbs of Sydney, Australia. If the pressing need for such pioneering models was not quite so obvious in the last decades of the twentieth century, it can hardly be avoided today in the ethnically diverse city in which Mathew continues to live and minister. Parkside Church meets in a suburb with over 60 different ethnic groups, and the congregation is a genuine reflection of the community's ethnic diversity. I've had the privilege of ministering there several times over the last decade: preaching, attending weddings and assisting in the ordination of a member of the pastoral team. On every occasion I have been deeply impressed by the delight that the congregation appears to find in their difference. It is impossible to imagine them meeting without overhearing conversations in multiple languages, contributing a bewildering range of meals for Sunday lunches in the church building, and yet worshipping together as one, with one voice, the one LORD. For Parkside Church, the otherworldly vision of Revelation 7 is becoming a present reality.

This book, then, is more than a theoretical discussion of a crucially important theme for the contemporary church. Mathew draws upon 30 years of leading a small, predominantly monoethnic church through several decades of solid and sustained growth, skilfully and patiently nurturing the ethnically diverse characteristics that is demonstrates today. But neither is this simply a descriptive case study. Mathew wants each of his readers to think carefully about the biblical and theological assumptions that are shaped by our backgrounds and upbringing and which are often uncritically inherited from our previous experiences of church. Here is a book that skilfully weaves case study, experience, biblical narrative and theological study in a form that allows its readers to continue their own journey of exploration through questions for personal reflection and enrichment.

Church without Borders is an inspiring book. I have been privileged to observe a very small part of the story of faithfulness and fruitfulness that make this book what it is: a multi-voiced witness that anticipates the praise of the Lamb by every tribe, people, nation and language. As you read it, I pray that you will discover the confidence to raise your voice alongside the differently accented voices of others, and together look forward with joy and celebration to taking your place among the heavenly throng assembled before the throne.

Rev. Dr Darrell Jackson
Associate Professor of Missiology, Morling College, Sydney, and the University of Divinity, Melbourne

Advent, 2018

CHURCH WITHOUT BORDERS

INTRODUCTION

Our world is changing.

Over the last century our world has seen two world wars. It has seen tyrants rise and fall, nuclear warfare, economic depressions, advancements in science and medicine, exploration into the frontiers of space, the birth of television, mobile phones, the internet and social media and the demarcating of more borders across the globe. Today we face many ethical questions around marriage equality, same-sex relationships, gender identity, abortion, euthanasia, mental illness, drug abuse, refugees, social media, cyber bullying, terrorism and climate change. In today's West, we are witnessing the slow decline of the Judeo-Christian worldview in favour of religious syncretism and New Age spirituality. Yet in the East and Africa, we see the rapid rise of Christian faith and the growth of churches.

In spite of all this change, Christ's commission to his followers remains unchanged.

> Then Jesus came to them and said, 'All authority in heaven and on earth has been given to me. Therefore go and make disciples of all nations, baptising them in the name of the Father and of the Son and of the Holy Spirit, and teaching them to obey everything I have commanded you. And surely I am with you always, to the very end of the age' (Matt 28:17–20).

The purpose of this book is to have a conversation about what it means to make disciples of all nations – and about the growing need for our churches, in this ever-changing world, to model the diversity of heaven in our local communities. It focuses on the theological mandate for multiethnic churches as well as the practical elements of building and nurturing a community composed of people from many ethnic backgrounds.

I, Mathew, have had the privilege of serving God for over thirty years in a multiethnic church setting. I have been Senior Pastor at Parkside Church, a community with over 60 different ethnicities. For many decades now, I have been part of a movement talking about the ever-growing need for our churches to be modelling the diversity we see in God's kingdom. For as Jesus said, 'My house will be called a house of prayer for all the nations' (Mark 11:17).

Today, especially in Australia, we are seeing church attendance drop – with the exception of multiethnic churches. In the past decade, we have seen incredible growth and renewed interest in churches that are reaching out to people from all different ethnic backgrounds. And why should we expect anything less, when heaven will be made up of people from every nation, tribe and tongue? God is calling his people to be a community that lives on earth 'as it is in heaven'.

Yet in spite of this, the sad reality of monocultural and monoethnic churches remains. Martin Luther King summarised it best when he said, '11 o'clock Sunday morning is the most segregated hour of the week ... and the Sunday school is still the most segregated school'.[1] According to leading research coming out of America, over 92 per cent of Catholic and Protestant churches are, to this day, monoethnic.[2]

Our world knows all too well the sadness caused by ethnic segregation. The past century is littered with examples: the anti-Semitic ideology and racial supremacy of Nazi Germany, which resulted in the deaths of over 60 million people and the extermination of approximately six million Jews in the Holocaust,[3] the civil rights movement in America, apartheid in South Africa; the caste system in India.[4] Closer to home, Australia has its own chequered history with the White Australia policy and our treatment of Indigenous Australians.

It is most troubling that during these times of ethnic division, the church hasn't always been the salt and light we are called to be.[5] Various branches of the church have at times been key players in fostering ethnic division. But God has called his people to be at the forefront of ethnic reconciliation. It remains the mission of the church to be the most diverse entity on the planet. We are called to be God's asylum – a *church without borders*, an asylum in which people from all walks of life and ethnic backgrounds can find salvation, peace, love and hope in God's sanctuary. For, as the Bible declares, 'My dwelling place also will be with them; and I will be their God, and they will be my people. And the nations will know that I am the Lord who sanctifies Israel, when my sanctuary is in their midst forever' (Ezek 37:27–28).

THE 'BOAT PEOPLE'

I have chosen to use the word 'asylum' as a deliberate metaphor. Discerning the meaning of asylum is a leading challenge for contemporary Australia. It relates to our policies on immigration and refugees, most notably around asylum seekers who travel by boat through people-smuggling operations. Such asylum seekers have been controversially dubbed the 'boat people'. This hot-button political issue has been fuelled by the ever-growing refugee crisis, which has emerged due to the growing rates of displaced people coming out of the Arab Spring crisis of 2011 and the internal turmoil of the Middle East.

Australia has always been a country built on immigration, from the Indigenous Australian population, who are believed to have migrated from South-East Asia some 40,000–45,000 years ago,[6] to the 1,300 or more passengers that arrived on the First Fleet in 1788.[7] Since October 1945, we have opened our doors to more than 7.5 million immigrants, over 800,000 of

INTRODUCTION

whom have been refugees or those entering under humanitarian programs. Our largest immigration intake came during the post-war period, when Australia welcomed more than 1.6 million migrants between October 1945 and June 1960.[8] By 1950, almost 200,000 displaced people from camps in Europe had been resettled on our shores.[9] Today, Australia is a signatory to the United Nations' 1951 *Convention Relating to the Status of Refugees* and its subsequent amendments.

Despite Australia's rich history on matters relating to immigration, the subject of refugees is one that sparks enormous controversy today. Since 1990, Australia has enforced a policy of mandatory detention for all asylum seekers. And since 2008, we have had over 50,000 asylum seeker arrivals without permit.[10]

With such statistical information behind us, it is fair to say that Australia has had a proud history of giving asylum to those in need. However, like the church, Australia could always be doing more to be an asylum for those refugees fleeing from great despair.

CHURCH AS ASYLUM

The church is God's asylum on earth. The church is a small representative of what God's future eternal asylum will be when Christ returns. This is an asylum filled with asylum seekers from every ethnicity under the sky.

This book explores the biblical and cultural mandates for multiethnic ministry as a basis and model for the Christian church. I argue that the church needs to strive towards establishing Christian communities that seek to model what heaven will look like. It is my belief, in line with the teachings of Christ, that one day heaven will be filled with people from every tongue, nation and tribe (Rev 7:9). I present a biblical case, hoping to inspire Christian leaders to adopt a multiethnic philosophy for their local church. I have not employed an overly sophisticated or highly academic style of writing, as I hope this book will be accessible to all individuals, regardless of biblical literacy.

The first chapter is devoted to telling you the story of how I came to faith and how my journey with God led me from India to Australia with the vision of establishing a multiethnic church for people of all nations. After this, the book is divided into three parts. Part 1 focuses on the mandate for multiethnic ministry, exploring some key texts. Part 2 zeroes in on Australia, exploring the cultural context for multiethnic ministry in our own backyard and a bit about our story at Parkside Church. Missionally speaking, Australia is a blessed country; God has brought people from every nation to our very doorstep. Therefore, I explore how the demographics of Australia have changed in recent decades and how this change needs to be reflected in the demographics of the church. Part 3 provides practical frameworks for building a multiethnic church. These chapters will be especially useful for Christian leaders and pastors seeking to grow a church in communities that have largely diverse populations. They will address questions such as how to turn a monoethnic church into a multiethnic church, what leadership needs to look like in that context and how to sustain such a church.

Before we begin the journey, we must create some working definitions of the important terms that will be used throughout the remainder of the book.

Multiethnic – A multiethnic church is composed of members of different ethnic backgrounds, gathered under one roof, using a common language to grow in the knowledge and love of Christ, while being intentional in pursuing God's mission to the world.

This definition is one I have applied for use at Parkside. A good friend of mine, Mark DeYmaz, in his book *Building a Healthy Multiethnic Church*, notes that the term multiethnic implies 'economic, educational, and generational diversity as well'.[11] In our view, therefore, multiethnic extends beyond just ethnic and national boundaries. It includes socio-economic, cultural, generational, political and educational diversity.

Another good friend and multiethnic advocate, Rodney Woo, in *The Color of the Church*, uses the synonym **multiracial** and applies this definition: 'The multiracial congregation is composed of racially diverse believers united by their faith in Christ, who make disciples of all nations in anticipation of the ultimate racial reunion around the throne'.[12]

Admittedly, I do prefer the term multiethnic to multiracial, because I believe that there is only one race – the human race. In Australia, people also tend towards political correctness and are concerned about how certain terms come across. Multiethnic seems to work better for our context.

Monoethnic – This relates to a church where most people in a congregation are primarily of one ethnic group. At times, the term monoethnic can be substituted for the academic term preferred by sociologists, 'homogenous'. Contrastingly, a multiethnic church is heterogeneous.

If you're interested in statistical definitions, then I refer you to the aforementioned research conducted in the United States in which over 92 per cent of churches are considered monoethnic, which means that over 80 per cent of the church is made up of people from one nation.[13] Accordingly, only around 7.5 per cent of churches in America are multiethnic; in those churches, no one group represents more than 80 per cent of the people. If we break it down even further, less than 12 per cent of Catholic churches and less than five per cent of evangelical churches can be classified as multiethnic.

Based on this research, American sociologist Michael Emerson defines a multiracial congregation as one where 'no one racial (ethnic) group is 80 per cent or more of the congregation'.[14]

This 80 per cent is not an arbitrary number. Rather, as Woo points out, the dynamics of a group change radically when there is a minority presence of over 20 per cent.[15]

Although I don't have any available statistical data for Australia, from my personal experience ministering in the context and talking to pastors and church leaders from across the country, I know very few churches that are operating under a multiethnic framework.

Right from the start, I'd like to clarify some other terms so as not to confuse anyone. Firstly, **multicultural** is one term I am reluctant to use to describe Parkside. In Australia, the word 'multiculturalism' arouses all kinds of fears, suspicions and negative feelings for many people. It is probably one of the most politicised and ill-defined concepts, and it carries kinds of negative connotations and stereotypes. Whenever someone uses the term multicultural, it tends to convey a perception (whether rightly or wrongly) that individuals would rather hold onto their own national identify and not conform to an Australian identity. Therefore, to avoid contention I steer well clear of it.

Further, multiethnic churches should not to be confused with **multilingual** churches. Some churches are multilingual in that they have different services to accommodate the various language groups in the church. Although they consider themselves one congregation, they divide the church into language-based congregations. For example, they might have a Mandarin speaking service to accommodate the Mandarin speakers and an English service to accommodate everyone else. Although I recognise that sometimes this can't be helped, especially for the first generation of migrants, I stress that this is not ideal for the longevity of the church, particularly for second and third generations. What makes multiethnic churches unique is that all different ethnicities and generations worship together at the same time.

Church – A church is simply any place where a group of Christians assemble and unite in worship of God. The design of the building is immaterial. Some people have preconceived ideas that it must have an altar, pews, and statues or stained-glass windows and must be some medieval-type cathedral or basilica. That is not the case; the church is a gathering of God's people not a building.

Asylum – In this book, the term asylum is a metaphor for the church. It is an all-inclusive refuge, welcoming people of all nations. The aim of the universal church throughout the entire world is to be an asylum whereby all humanity can seek refuge in God's house. Practically speaking, when you or I walk into a church we should expect the church and its members to model – not perfectly, but in some ways – what heaven will look like. A church is not a club but a place for all of God's people – regardless of ethnicity, gender or socio-economics – to worship God together.

Asylum seeker – This term is usually used to describe individuals who are forced out of their homeland for any number of possible reasons and seek sanctuary in a foreign country. I have taken the contemporary term and applied it to every human being. We are all asylum seekers – refugees in the quest for a sanctuary only God can offer.

CHAPTER 1
ONE ASYLUM SEEKER AMONG THE MANY

In the early chapters of the book of Exodus, we see God at work behind the scenes, orchestrating the events of Moses' life. While the Israelites were being unfavourably treated in public policy, Moses' mother placed him in a papyrus vessel and sent him down the Nile (Exod 2:3). Moses is a different kind of refugee, placed in a 'boat', given asylum in the very house of the one persecuting his people.

What is powerful about Moses' story is the way God prepared him for the future task at hand – liberating his people. God orchestrated things so that Moses would have an Egyptian upbringing, an Egyptian education and Egyptian military training – all skills he would have used later in life during Israel's liberation. Moses had no idea about the bigger plan God had for his life. The oppressed Israelites had no idea of the bigger plan God had for them. Even as God liberated them from Egypt, Moses and the Israelites remained unware of the plans God had for them: to form them into a great nation from whom, one day, a great liberator for all people would come!

My asylum story begins in the distant and remote village community of Kerala in India. Today, Kerala is a popular tourist destination, located in the south-west region of India. It is a tropical maritime region, renowned for its breathtaking, natural beauty: sky-scraping mountain ranges with lush greenery, picture-perfect palm trees and plantations, placid lakes, a vast expanse of regal beaches and the peaceful yet riveting backwaters. Kerala, 'the land of 44 rivers', has built a reputation of being 'God's own country'.

In comparison to other parts of India, Kerala is diversified. According to 2011 census data, the population is 54.73 per cent Hindu, 26.56 per cent Islamic and 18.38 per cent Christian.[16] Overall Christianity, although the third largest religion in India with approximately 24 million followers, remains a small minority, a little over two per cent.[17] The traditional view is that Christianity began in India around 52 AD with the arrival of Thomas, who brought the gospel message to Jewish settlers in Kerala.[18] Officially, the Indian constitution grants freedom of religion.[19] However, throughout the years there have been numerous examples of anti-Christian violence, and in some areas the persecution shows an alarming breach of human rights. Several church leaders have noted that the attacks on Christians have increased throughout the terms of the Hindu-nationalist Bharatiya Janata Party.

In the India in which I grew up, Christianity had been influenced by a caste system for many centuries. In India, the caste system is a form of social stratification, classifying certain people groups based on socio-economic factors. The classifications are generationally binding and rooted in religion, with those of the lowest castes frequently experiencing discrimination and social segregation. These societal rankings class people into four main categories: the highest echelon is made up of the priests and scholars, followed by the nobility, governors and military, then the merchants, skilled artisans and argriculturalists, and at the bottom are the unskilled labourers. Last, not even worthy of being categorised, ostracised by other caste groups, are the Untouchables (referred to as Dalits, meaning 'supressed') and Other Backward Classes.

The Untouchables were regarded as unclean because of their association with working in manual labour jobs that were considered polluted, such as cleaning toilets, removal of waste and handling animal carcasses. The attitude was that they were primitive people, and as a result the Untouchables were segregated and banned from schools, education, temples, water wells and participation in everyday society. Despite modern reforms to India, today the Untouchables are still very prominent, with as many as 400 million people living below the international poverty line. Most of these are Dalits, who live on the streets as beggars and are at enormous risk of human trafficking, forced labour and commercial sex exploitation.

The role of the church in such a culture can often be muddied. External organisations and charities like World Vision strive desperately to aid these underprivileged communities. There are also individual missionaries like Mother Teresa who have worked with those most impoverished over many years. Amazingly about 80 per cent of the Christian population of India is made up of those from the poorest and lowest class.

In many ways, however, the church's response to the caste system in India has frequently reflected the same social segregation of the nation. In Kerala, for instance, certain pockets of Syrian Christians attempted to maintain their noble status. This resulted in members using ritual bathing for cleansing purposes to purify themselves when encountering someone from an inferior class. Some congregations have rejected partnering with foreign missionary organisations working with Untouchables and prevented converts from a lower caste joining their church or intermarrying with those outside the caste.

The Catholic Church has been something of a better example than other religious institutions in their treatment of lower castes. Nevertheless, there have been cases of separate congregations, separate seats, separate communion cups and separate burial grounds being accorded to those of lesser castes. The higher castes control the majority of church leadership roles. Most priests and nuns are from the higher castes, despite the overwhelmingly high ratio of Dalits in the Christian population.

The issue is still so prevalent that upon a visit to India in 2003, Pope John Paul II was critical of the Church's caste discrimination, stating: 'It is the Church's obligation to work unceasingly to change hearts, helping all people to see every human being as a child of God, a brother or sister of Christ, and therefore a member of our own family'.[20]

The only logical thing one can ask is, how is this system of church any different to that experienced in the time of Christ? During the first century AD, there were members of the Jewish elite, members of the Pharisaic and Sanhedrin orders, who looked unfavourably towards non-Jews and the poorer members of society – the widows, the orphans, the disabled, the lepers and so on. The Jewish temple had a separate precinct, known as the Court of the Gentiles, where non-Jewish people could worship. Non-Jews were forbidden from entering the temple itself. Those with leprosy were expelled from the community. People from the north, the Samaritans, were regarded as an unclean race – they had intermarried with foreign women and consequently become 'racially impure'. As was not uncommon in the ancient world, whole groups, whether they be women or slaves, were disadvantaged and not given equal opportunities. Sometimes particular occupations, like shepherds, butchers and sailors, carried certain stereotypes because of the 'dishonourable' perceptions about the nature of their work. At times, this could impact their ability to provide legal testimony. The comparisons between the caste system in India and the first-century AD context are obvious. Even in modern society, we see examples of such oppression.

I want to stress the point that none of this is God's doing. It is people doing such things, packaging it in the form of religious devotion. God's intention is for all people to have a place before him. For God declares, 'My house will be called a house of prayer for all nations' (Isa 56:7).

What's sad is that the church is supposed to be above all societal segregation, a place where all asylum seekers are welcomed and embraced as part of God's family. If the church cannot become a place for people of all nations, then don't expect any other secular institution to achieve such a vision. If Christian leaders are unwilling to step up and embrace a multiethnic vision for their church, then how does the church truly expect to live out its calling to be an all-inclusive asylum?

Returning to my story, I grew up in a devout Catholic family. My dad owned a coffee plantation, and he employed people from a variety of cultural backgrounds. So, from the very beginning I was exposed to a cross-cultural set up. We were very religious people. My parents would enforce mandatory church attendance, but there was never a personal relationship with God. Throughout my teenage years, I was not interested in school, so I used to get up to mischief. My parents resorted to sending me to a variety of different schools because I would get into trouble.

At the age of fifteen, I became a committed Christian. It was upon realising that I could have a personal relationship with the living God, who created the heavens and the earth, that I developed a real conviction to communicate the gospel message with other people. Subsequently, I joined the well-known missionary group, Operation Mobilisation. I began taking the gospel message to different parts of India and was immediately thrown into a whole other cross-cultural set up. I remember having to learn other languages in order to preach. This was a real eye-opening experience. I envisioned that one could just go out and preach to people about Jesus and everyone would simply accept the message. However, this was far from the case. On one occasion, I was attacked and hospitalised by a group of fanatical Hindus. This did little to discourage me; rather, it strengthened my resolve. I quickly realised that if people were opposing my message, then there must be something real and something valuable driving it.

Afterwards, I had the opportunity to serve aboard Operation Mobilisation's missionary ship, *Logos*. *Logos* is a ship that travels throughout the world, sharing the gospel message, distributing Christian literature, providing relief and encouraging cross-cultural communication. Since the 1970s, OM teams have visited more than 480 ports in over 150 countries.

The fifteen months I spent on board *Logos* was a defining period. It profoundly opened my eyes to God's global mission and his desire to create a church made up of people from all nations. We were a group of people from 35 different countries, all sharing space and eating together on one small ship. If you didn't break down those racial barriers and you didn't get along, you had no choice but to jump overboard. In my cabin, I was rooming with one Danish and one Scottish guy. At the best of times, travelling with people you are related to is hard enough. After a while you tend to get sick of each other's company. Not only were we 35 different nationalities living together, but every week we were travelling to another country or city. What united us was our passion for Christ and our sole aim to spread the gospel. In total, we visited over 30 countries and attracted a great deal of attention. It is not every day that a group of volunteers from so many different nationalities arrives at a port. We stood out.

Everything we did was multiethnic, whether it was overnight prayer teams gathering together and praying in different languages or going out in small teams to different village communities. The language barrier never impeded our ability to work and serve God together, so why should it affect any church today? Not only did I have the privilege of getting to know the people on board the ship, but every week we were visiting another country, mixing with the locals, experiencing different cultures, eating diverse foods. It was an exhilarating experience, and I soon realised something. Wouldn't it be wonderful if there could be a church like this? A church where people of all nations could worship God together – a multiethnic church!

From the *Logos*, I travelled back to India and started teaching in the north-east in the state of Manipur. Now these schools were made up of tribal people from so many different tribal groups who had come together in one area. This was remarkable because, I suppose, much like the explosion of missionaries that went out during the 1800s, it dawned on me that God cares about and has a plan for people we might consider primitive.

For so many years, the church had fallen into the same game that society had collapsed into. When the mindset is that certain people are considered of lower class, the church tends to follow that principle and establish churches to reach certain demographics. I remember on one occasion visiting a church service in the US and being told by someone that I would feel more comfortable going across the road to a black church, where I could be more relaxed around people like myself. Apart from the fact that I'm not African-American, I suppose he thought that because I had brown skin, I would fit in. It was discouraging to discover this sort of attitude.

It was out of my tribal setting that I came to Sydney, Australia. My objective was to learn more about tribal ministry and get some training on how to effectively reach different tribal people. I couldn't have imagined how, several years later, God would place me as the pastor of a multiethnic church in the Western region of Sydney, Australia. It was just God's way of grooming me for the mission ahead.

During this period, an exciting thing happened to me. I met my future wife, Savi. I was moving between Sydney and the US for my training in tribal ministry and linguistics. In the process, I visited Fiji, which is where we met. Fiji was a fresh experience for me. Prior to my visit, I hadn't even heard of the collection of remote islands in the South Pacific Ocean that make up Fiji. The nation has a rich tribal history of warring tribes, cannibalism and many languages and cultures, dating from ancient times right up to European colonisation.

Savi and I shared a desire to serve God in the mission field. Accordingly, we both pursued our studies, her in Australia and me in the States. For two years, we communicated via letter. In August 1979 we married, and in 1981 we welcomed our first child, our daughter Sherina. Two years later, our son Jason was born. These years of trying to build our marriage and raise the kids were incredibly hectic. I was completing my theological training at Morling Bible College in Sydney. There was no internet during those days, so we couldn't look things up online to complete an assignment; we had to sift through books and concordances. Nevertheless, we got through. After pastoring churches in Yagoona and Maroubra in the South-West and Eastern Suburbs of Sydney respectively, we accepted a role at Parkside Church in the Western region of Sydney.

I have dedicated a later chapter to discussing the story of Parkside Church and how it grew into the church it is today. Ultimately, the longevity of our ministry has resulted from God's faithfulness and the desire he placed on both our lives to pastor a multiethnic church. Throughout the earliest stages of our marriage, he ignited a burning passion in our hearts that his desire for us was to build a church that would be recognised as a safe asylum for all people, regardless of their racial background.

When we look to the future, we see some incredible challenges for the universal church throughout the entire world. Christianity is on the decline. At least in the Western world, the Christian voice is becoming marginalised. Today in Australia, around half the population still affiliate themselves with Christianity, but according to recent census data this is on the way down.[21] This can be seen in the rapid decline in church attendance.[22] We have also seen the rise of those identifying themselves as 'spiritual but not religious', or of no religious affiliation whatsoever. Surveys indicate that although many people still see themselves as having some spiritual side, most don't see God as playing a major role in their daily lives.[23] Moreover, such trends are resulting in the Christian voice dying out on contemporary ethical issues like abortion, same-sex marriages and euthanasia.

What's the solution? There is no doubt that Christians and churches could be doing a multitude of things differently in the world, and I wouldn't want to be too simplistic about solutions to the church's decline in the West. Nevertheless, the church needs to become better at once more representing the issues people in the community are experiencing. That certainly begins with reflecting the diversity of the communities around us.

In Australia, this includes re-educating ourselves about God's original purpose for the church. In Part 1, we're going to explore God's intended purpose and mandate for the church. It is a mandate that takes the very fabric of society, the foundations of order, and completely flips it over, turning what we know about humankind on its head. It is a vision for a church filled with asylum seekers, a vision in which all people throughout the entire human history could seek asylum in the refuge of God. The church was designed to be a place which modelled the sanctuary of God, on earth as it is in heaven – a church without borders.

QUESTIONS FOR DISCUSSION

1. What attracted you to the local church(es) you have been a part of? How does this affect your present understanding of the biblical model of a multiethnic church?

2. How does your understanding of the character of God shape your understanding of God's church?

PART 1:
UNDERSTANDING THE ASYLUM

CHAPTER 2
JESUS THE ASYLUM SEEKER

When Martin Luther King made his 'I Have a Dream' speech, now entrenched in the chronicles of history, and declared the equality of all men to be 'self-evident', I doubt any member of the crowd turned to the person next to them in bewilderment and asked, 'Are all people really created equal?' Of course not. That turn of phrase was, and still is, deeply rooted in the American psyche. King's aspiration was to call the American people back to their roots, back to the very foundations upon which American society was built – equality for all people. King declared this benchmark and asked the people for an assessment as to whether American society had been living up to the standards it had set for itself on 4 July 1776.

Much in the same way, this first part of the book will be devoted to calling the church and its leaders back to the foundation, back to the benchmark Christ set out on that celebrated day when he left us in charge of the mission.

Throughout the following chapters, we will assess the biblical mandate for multiethnic ministry, exploring why adopting a multiethnic framework is not only the biblical directive but also the only type of church you and I can expect to see in heaven. We shall examine several key biblical texts, identifying:

1. God's vision for a multiethnic asylum (Isa 56:7)

2. A practical example of a multiethnic asylum in the New Testament (Acts 11:19-30)

3. The greatest multiethnic asylum depicted in the Bible (Rev 7:9)

Before we get there, we're going to spend this chapter redefining our understanding of what it means to be an asylum seeker by looking at some characters from the Bible.

If I had my way, I'd prefer to avoid terms like multiethnic, multicultural or international completely when describing the church. When people think of the Christian church, images of multiethnicity and diversity should be automatically invoked. When people think of Jesus, the first image that usually comes to minds is the cross. And when people think of *church*, they should think of Jesus and the diversity of those who are part of his kingdom. After all God's asylum, his kingdom, is multiethnic. As such, Jesus has called the church to model multiethnicity 'on earth as it is in heaven' (Matt 6:10). The church is not only entrusted with the responsibility of preaching the gospel; it is called to be an 'anticipatory sign' of that which is to come.[24] The church is a small reflection of a higher reality. In God's kingdom, there is diversity, and this should be mirrored in the church.

Consequently, the goal of this section is to challenge leaders to recognise that the aim of the local church community is to mirror the diversity of heaven. Our desire should never be to run a church which primarily caters for people of our ethnic likeness. The long-term vision of a church community should never strive to be homogenous.[25]

JESUS THE REFUGEE

There can be a lot of negative publicity directed towards refugees. In Australia and around the world, the media uses all sorts of terms to describe people who come looking for refuge: asylum seekers, refugees, displaced people, queue jumpers, illegal immigrants, economic refugees, boat people. We need to broaden our definitions.

In Australia, societal attitudes towards refugees are complex. Asylum seekers are a product of the wider ethnic divisions the world experiences. These divides extend beyond race to include things such as gender, socio-economics, politics and ideologies. The distrust of asylum seekers is heightened when other fears like terrorism and national security get thrown into the mix. Additionally, governments and people are also fearful of experiencing an influx of refugees from a culture so different to the Western culture. This fear has been heightened by examples of poor integration of such influxes in Europe. From these rapid waves, cultural ghettos develop, and nations must wrestle with the societal changes and integrative challenges that emerge. Sadly, for some countries bound by economic constraints, there's just no way to cope with the financial strain. Assimilating new arrivals is an impossible task and adds more pressure to the already burdened local community. The task is made more complicated when differing political ideologies disagree about the most effective approaches to tackling these challenges. Sometime this can't be helped, as governments need to prioritise the more immediate concerns of their public.

With this current backdrop, it is prudent to recognise that the Christian worldview is not devoid of meaningful thought on the subject of asylum seekers. When viewed through a particular lens, we can notice that the Bible is full of asylum seeker stories. In fact, the most famous person in history, Jesus, was an asylum seeker.

Here is how the Bible describes Jesus:

> He came to that which was his own, but his own did not receive him (John 1:1).

> He was despised and rejected by mankind, a man of suffering, and familiar with pain. Like one from whom people hide their faces he was despised, and we held him in low esteem (Isa 53:3).

Jesus was born in the first century into an area of political turmoil not too dissimilar from the war-ravaged parts of today's world. When we think of areas synonymous with war and asylum seekers – whether the Middle East today or Europe during the first half of the twentieth century – the Roman province Jesus was born into, Judea, conjures the same sorts of associations. The whole region of ancient Israel has, throughout its history, been subject to wars and conquests, revolts and subjugation. In the centuries leading up to Jesus' birth, the kingdom was conquered by the Assyrians, the Babylonians and the Greeks, and eventually came under Roman rule. Even under Roman rule, the area was a hotbed for rebellions, with client kings like Herod the Great (and his children) and prefects like Pontius Pilate entrusted with trying to maintain order. Infighting among different groups conspiring to hold their own share of influence and political power contributed to instability. Some of these influential groups – Pharisees, Sadducees and Zealots – are found in the Gospel texts. Eventually, when the revolts grew out of hand in 70 AD, the Romans besieged Jerusalem and destroyed the city, killing many and enslaving the rest.

Today, we know that asylum seekers are coming out of areas where there is a large power vacuum. The contemporary crises in the Middle East are impacted by the toppling of former regimes and dictators, especially since the Arab Spring of 2011. The term 'Arab Spring' refers to a series of revolutionary waves – protests, riots, social violence and civil wars – that have engulfed nations in the Middle East and North Africa since

2010. Major uprisings and insurgencies have engulfed Tunisia, Egypt, Libya, Yemen, Syria and Iraq. Different terrorist groups and rebel armies in Iraq and Syria especially have capitalised on the situation. Other Arab nations to experience sustained demonstrations include Algeria, Bahrain, Iran, Jordan, Kuwait, Lebanon, Morocco, Oman and Sudan.

We must view the world Jesus grew up in much like our own. When we look at the early years of Jesus' life, he fits the definition of what we would call an asylum seeker today. Jesus spent the early years of his life as a displaced person, fleeing from political persecution. After his birth (around 4 BC), Jesus' family were forced to flee from Bethlehem to Egypt because Herod the Great, in an attempt to shore up his power, threatened Jesus' safety (Matt 2:1–18). Even after Herod died, the family had to alter their plans to return to Israel, heading instead to the town they were originally from (Nazareth in Galilee) because Herod's son Archelaus possessed an equal lust for blood (Matt 2:19–23). The historian Josephus gives us the context for this plight. Around this time, there was an uprising in the temple during Passover in Jerusalem. In the process, a group of Roman soldiers were killed. Archelaus cancelled Passover, slaughtering many Jews and sending the other pilgrims home.[26]

It is possible Jesus was borrowing from his early life experience when he remarked, 'Foxes have dens and birds have nests, but the Son of Man has no place to lay his head' (Luke 9:58).

Moreover, we could understand Jesus' entire life as an asylum seeker story. Jesus' very entry into the world from heaven to earth – what Christians call 'the incarnation' – makes him a refugee. He left his home, his eternal dwelling, to come and live in a foreign land. The jump Jesus made was immeasurably greater than that of any asylum seeker. Jesus is the Immanuel, the God with us. Jesus is the Asylum Seeker with us, among us.

Jesus came into the world to set people free: 'The Spirit of the LORD is on me, because he has anointed me to proclaim good news to the poor. He has sent me to proclaim freedom for the prisoners and recovery of sight for the blind, to set the oppressed free ...' (Luke 4:18).

Those words are so powerful. Jesus is daring to set the captives free. Whether or not we realise it, we are all captives. The Bible says we are captives to sin (Rom 6:20). We are slaves to sin who have been set free by Jesus.

ASYLUM SEEKERS OF THE BIBLE

Many hundreds of years before Jesus, we were introduced to the story of Noah (Gen 6—9:29) and how his story was that of an asylum seeker. Noah's ark was a safe asylum, a vessel designed to protect Noah and his family. Today, thousands of refugees seek asylum in order to protect themselves from the terror that sweeps their homeland. Some dash across borders into other nations, while others like Noah use a vessel to flee across the ocean. You could say Noah's family were the first 'boat people'.

Afterwards in Genesis, we are introduced to a Bedouin man from Mesopotamia. Historically the Bedouin, translated 'wanderer', were desert-dwelling nomadic people who lived in tents throughout the Middle East. The Bedouin were indigenous people, who traditionally lived off the land, engaging in agriculture, herding, hunting and fishing. Scarce water supplies and pastoral lands meant that they were on the move constantly. Although the numbers have significantly declined over the twentieth century, the Bedouin are still prominent in parts of the Middle East including Saudi Arabia, Jordan, Israel, Egypt and Syria. They are known to be some of the most hospitable people on the planet.

This particular Bedouin was called Abraham. God made an extraordinary promise to Abraham. He promised this Bedouin that from him all nations, all people on the planet, would be blessed.

> I will surely bless you and make your descendants as numerous as the stars in the sky and as the sand on the seashore. Your descendants will take possession of the cities of their enemies, and through your offspring all nations on earth will be blessed, because you have obeyed me (Gen 22:17–18).

Remarkable, isn't it? From this Bedouin, the Untouchable in India would be blessed. From this Bedouin, the Indigenous Australian would be blessed. The Jewish Holocaust victim, the tribal chief living in the remotest community in the globe, the Hispanic American, the persecuted believer in China – all peoples would be blessed! But Abraham was just an asylum seeker. He would be called by God to leave his homeland of Ur in the Chaldean Empire in Mesopotamia. He would travel to Haran and into the lands of Canaan and on into Shechem (around the region of the West Bank), Bethel (near modern day Jerusalem) and eventually Egypt.

Another powerful example was Abraham's great grandson Joseph, whose story occupies the lion's share of chapters 37 to 50 in the book of Genesis. As a young boy, Joseph was shunned by his family, which in those days was like been made 'stateless', and sold into slavery. After being sent to Egypt, Joseph found himself imprisoned for a time. Through a miraculous change of fortune, he then rose to become the highest official in Egypt, appointed by Pharaoh as vizier. For Joseph to achieve so much, after such a tumultuous early life, was momentous. It can in some ways can be compared to the momentousness of African Americans finally having a black president. It is also a powerful testimony to what God can do with people rejected by society.

Then there was Moses. During his mid-life, fearing for his life, Moses fled from Egypt to live in the desert in Midian (northwest Arabian Peninsula). The desert became his 'asylum' – until God sent him back to Egypt with a greater mission. The very people Moses returned to, the Israelites, were asylum seekers also. After centuries of slavery in Egypt, God through Moses set the Israelites free. They then spent 40 years wandering the desert awaiting entry to the promised asylum, the land of

Canaan. During this period, the Israelites lived in tents, under Moses' leadership. Amazingly, unlike the nations around them, the God of Israel lived in a tent, known as the tabernacle, just like his people.

Let's not forget Israel's most renowned King – David. David absconded from his palace in Jerusalem to seek refuge in the desert when his life was threatened by his own son, Absalom (2 Sam 15–19). This wasn't the first time David had to flee to the desert, seeking political asylum. Before he became king, his predecessor Saul feared David's ambition and sought his life (1 Sam 18–21). Reflecting on the peril of this experience, David sang this beautiful line: 'The LORD is my rock, my fortress and my deliverer; my God is my rock, in whom I take refuge, my shield and the horn of my salvation, my stronghold' (Ps 18:2).

This is the song of a refugee, singing about his search for refuge and finding it in God.

Elsewhere, David would sing that most beautiful psalm about forever dwelling in God's asylum: 'And I will dwell in the house of the LORD for ever' (Ps 23:6).

But our narrative continues. In 586 BC, Jerusalem was destroyed, and the people of Israel were sent into exile, once again finding themselves under oppression and in need of asylum. The people spent 70 years living in exile in a foreign land before the asylum seekers were finally sent back home under the Persian foreign policy in 539 BC (2 Chron 36:22–23). But even in Babylon, the prophet Ezekiel made it known that

God didn't dwell in some temple, but that God had come with the asylum seekers into exile (see Ezekiel 1).

The theme can continue. You have Ruth, who left her home for humanitarian reasons, due to risk of famine. Daniel, Shadrach, Meshach and Abednego were all young men, swooped up by the invading Babylonian army and forced to leave their homeland.

The asylum story continues in the New Testament. After the stoning of a Christian convert named Stephen, a great wave of persecution forced many in the early church to seek asylum beyond their ancestral homeland, Jerusalem (Acts 7—8:3). But, as was the case with all these asylum stories, God used their refugee status for his purposes, for his salvation. Out of this wave of persecution, the church grew into the multiethnic movement we know today: 'Those who had been scattered preached the word wherever they went' (Acts 8:4).

SEVEN BILLION ASYLUM SEEKERS

The United Nations High Commissioner for Refugees (UNHCR) currently estimates that there are some 65 million forcibly displaced persons globally. These can be either refugees who have fled their country or those who are classified as 'internally displaced' (ID), meaning they are displaced but remain within their own country. About 22.5 million of these, half of whom are under the age of 18, have formal recognition of some sorts with the UNHCR. Around 38 million can be categorised as ID, with around 10 million considered 'stateless', according to UN recognition. Over 60 per cent of internally displaced persons are from Congo, Iraq, Nigeria, South Sudan and Syria. More than 40 per cent of Syria's population is now internally displaced due to the long-standing crisis. And more than 55 per cent of refugees come from Syria, South Sudan and Afghanistan. Mainly due to their proximity, Turkey, Pakistan, Lebanon, Iran, Uganda, Ethiopia and Jordan are the top hosting countries, while America, Canada, Australia, Sweden, Norway and the UK are among the top countries used for resettlement.[27]

The greatest challenge for asylum seekers, as Australia has always known, is resettlement and integration. In the post-World War II period, most refugees to Australia were from devastated parts of Europe. Around thirty years ago, they were from Asian nations like Vietnam and Cambodia. As any person who has migrated to another country can tell you, it can be difficult enough trying to learn another language, find employment, make friends, buy a house and learn the ropes of that society. It is made immensely more difficult when you're doing it not by choice, but out of a necessity to survive. In most cases, asylum seekers have suffered great loss and relocate without the rest of their family.

With all the difficulties the world has with resettling just 65 million asylum seekers, imagine if, in the world, there were over 7.5 *billion* asylum seekers – and counting. Experts agree that the population is increasing by about 70 million per year, which equates to around 140 more people every minute, or 200,000 per day. To put that in perspective, if the Australian population is just over 24 million, you're almost tripling our population each and every year. It is unfathomable. By the time this book is published, the quoted figure of 7.5 billion will be obsolete.

If everybody in the world was an asylum seeker, there's another important question to ask. Who is responsible for all those people? Actually, there is someone who holds sovereignty over that many asylum seekers – God. God is present for every single birth, every single death, every single victory, defeat, laugh, cry – every single breath. He's there for every single asylum seeker. He knows every single asylum seeker better than they know themselves.

But the scary thing is, in his grace, God created an organisation to help him in the care for the billions of asylum seekers. Jesus called it his *ekklesia* (Matt 16:18); today, we call it the church. Jesus didn't invent the term *ekklesia*. Rather, the word was already in colloquial use to refer to an assembly or public gathering (Acts 19:39).[28] The term then took on a whole other meaning for the early Christians, especially once the Apostle Paul got a hold of it. Subsequently, the church has been commissioned with the task of gathering all people who are seeking eternity and refuge in the Creator. The church is charged with gathering all asylum seekers to the one eternal asylum. The church is charged with the task of teaching, edifying and discipling all asylum seekers to know the good news about Jesus' death and resurrection and how to be a faithful citizen of the kingdom of God. We are God's servants, his asylum seekers, given the mission of reaching other asylum seekers.

With such a rich mission, it shouldn't surprise us that when we search the Scriptures, what we find is just one big asylum seeker story. Much has been written about God's everlasting care for all people, regardless of race, colour, gender or socio-economics. Therefore, our emphasis will not be on repeating that. Neither will our emphasis be on communicating *why* we should be reaching people from all nations. Jesus saves us the time in that most famous commission:

> Then Jesus came to them and said, 'All authority in heaven and on earth has been given to me. Therefore, go and make disciples of all nations, baptising them in the name of the Father and of the Son and of the Holy Spirit, and teaching them to obey everything I have commanded you. And surely, I am with you always, to the very end of the age' (Matt 28:17–20).

When Jesus looked into the world, he had compassion because we were like a wandering, unprotected flock: 'For "you were like sheep going astray", but now you have returned to the Shepherd and Overseer of your souls' (1 Pet 2:25). Jesus wanted to leave no doubt about what he wanted from his church.

But sometimes I wonder whether the church has overcomplicated this commission. When you walk into a church that is predominantly made up of one ethnicity, you have to question whether or not that church has missed something.

The Bible is not a book of mythology or mere philosophy, but a story that the everyday man or woman can relate to. It is the greatest story ever told, because it is a story that all people can feel affinity with. The Bible is a history of those asylum seekers gone before us and the 7.5 billion asylum seekers (and counting) today.

'STOP THE BOATS!'

'The foreigner residing among you must be treated as your native-born. Love them as yourself, for you were foreigners in Egypt. I am the LORD your God' (Lev 19:34).

Throughout this book, we need to discuss possible objections people might have to multiethnic churches. Before going any further, it is helpful to place a few markers for those within the church who are sceptical of the need to become multiethnic.

As noted, resettling refugees presents a challenge to any nation. Although international law sets out certain guidelines that must be followed, individual nations must still administer effective policies. This can be immensely difficult, especially when the world finds itself amid a refugee crisis like the present Syrian situation. The asylum seeker count grows day by day.

When it comes to the effectiveness of resettlement, Australia is an interesting example. Their focus is on stopping people smugglers from taking advantage of genuine refugees. Politically, this is a highly controversial and emotive issue.

There are many on the other side, who believe Australia is failing in its humanitarian obligations towards refugees. The government's offshore processing centres and campaigns to deter people-smuggling operations have attracted much scrutiny. Many nations, seeking to avoid some of the drama emerging in European nations, have praised Australia's approach. Others have criticised the government's response as being too harsh and an embarrassment.

Critical to a nation's approach is the philosophy that undergirds its policy. You could say that Leviticus 19:34 was Israel's philosophical approach. This was the statement that was supposed to govern the way Israel treated foreigners. In Australia, the political slogan 'stop the boats' has been a popular but controversial way for the government in recent years to articulate its philosophical approach to treating foreigners, which is focused on stopping people smugglers from taking advantage of genuine refugees.

It is with a little tongue-in-cheek, then, that I want to give some food for thought to those who advocate monocultural churches and may wish to 'stop the boat' before our multiethnic vessel gets underway.

In an article defending the monoethnic church movement, Tom Steers made this statement: 'But despite what some advocates imply, multicultural ministry is not more biblical, let alone always most effective. I think our multicultural situation demands that we also employ what I call a monocultural approach'.[29]

The logic of Steers' argument reflects that of other monoethnic church proponents. Steers believes multiethnic churches are primarily a response to the changing cultural dynamics of American society. He claims that the growing diversity of society instead points to a greater need for more monoethnic churches. Citing some thirty years of experience, Steers notes that multiethnic church structures can be a great hindrance to new migrants, who typically face many struggles when assimilating into a new society. He maintains that establishing monoracial churches is the most effective way to remove barriers to conversion for these new migrants, allowing the gospel to filter from these migrants to their families. Furthermore, he cites as his model the approach of Jesus, who did most of his messianic work within the Jewish context.

Naturally, the reader may have guessed that I passionately disagree with the main premise of this article. There will be those who, although advocating the need for more monoethnic churches, have a more nuanced argument than Steers. Irrespective, I find the theological justification for monoethnic churches to be seriously lacking. While I want to affirm that those who advocate for the establishment of monoethnic churches are our co-workers in the gospel, I believe it helpful to offer a response to their approach.

First, while Jesus' ministry was primarily directed towards the Jews, his Great Commission was not. That was directed to reaching all humanity, Jews and Gentiles, without discrimination. What's more, although it is important to observe closely the life of Jesus and extrapolate principles for imitation, there are areas of Jesus' ministry that diverge from our own. The best example for this is Jesus' sacrificial death. The atonement component of Jesus' mission was something that only he could complete. We are not called to repeat that, only celebrate it and share in it by picking up our cross to follow him.

The same can be said for Jesus' 'first to the Jew then to the Gentile' and 'I was sent only to the lost sheep of Israel' missional approach (Matt 15:24; see Rom 1:16). In Christ, God sought to fulfil his promises to Israel from old. As a result, the proclamation of the messianic message and the coming kingdom was directed first to the lost sheep of Israel (Matt 10:5–6), before expanding to include the Gentiles. God's original selection of Israel was not about race or ethnicity. It was part of his grand plan for the salvation of humankind (Deut 7:7–8).

In addition to this, we are told by the historian Josephus that Jesus' movement 'won over both many Jews and many Greeks'.[30] This debunks any idea that Jesus' mission was, or was at least interpreted by his followers to be, exclusive to the Jews. In fact, the two people Jesus praised for having the greatest faith were not native Israelites (see Matt 15:21–28; Luke 7:1–10).

Further, citing Jesus' statement about lost sheep (Matt 15:24) as evidence for why monoethnic churches are the most theologically sound approach fails to consider the whole witness of Scripture. Part of Jesus' evangelistic approach was to reshape the existing attitudes of those around him. In the context of Matthew 15, Jesus was challenging the attitudes of those around him who thought his messianic mission was *only* available to the Jews. The Canaanite woman understood this, and Jesus praised her for her faith.

Some might suggest that the calling of Peter and James as apostles to the Jews and Paul as apostle to the Gentiles (Gal 2:7–9) is evidence that some may be called to monoethnic church settings. This is to confuse evangelism with the congregational church setting. The issue at hand in Galatia (see Acts 15 and the book of Galatians) is fellowship. The centre of the issue is the question, 'Who belongs at the table of fellowship in Christ?' For Paul, this cuts at the very heart of the gospel message. In Galatians, as is the case in Acts 15, there are some who argued that, for a believer to truly belong to Christ, they must also be circumcised. For Paul, this is nonsense, because we are justified by faith, not by keeping certain boundary markers. In Paul's mind, all are justified through the same mechanism and therefore equal before Christ. Accordingly, any nationality markers are in one sense stripped away because of grace. Therefore, Paul challenges Peter when he comes to Antioch (see Galatians 2). Paul in effect says to Peter, 'Because we are all on the same footing, it is foolish to split the church up into different ethnic camps'.

> After much discussion, Peter got up and addressed them: 'Brothers, you know that some time ago God made a choice among you that the Gentiles might hear from my lips the message of the gospel and believe. God, who knows the heart, showed that he

> accepted them by giving the Holy Spirit to them, just as he did to us. He did not discriminate between us and them, for he purified their hearts by faith. Now then, why do you try to test God by putting on the necks of Gentiles a yoke that neither we nor our ancestors have been able to bear? No! We believe it is through the grace of our Lord Jesus that we are saved, just as they are' (Acts 15:7–11).

> Here there is no Gentile or Jew, circumcised or uncircumcised, barbarian, Scythian, slave or free, but Christ is all, and is in all (Col 3:11).

As identifiable pillars in their respective groups – Peter and James to the Jews and Paul to the Gentile churches he'd planted – they were sent away with that exact message.

Second, and closely related to this point (as I argue in Appendix 1) a monoethnic mission strategy that seeks to eliminate barriers to conversion through homogenous churches is simply a misapplication of the homogenous unit principle. This does not mean that local churches need not be considerate of the cultural obstacles that may hinder new believers. What it does stress is that we cannot forfeit our eternal identity simply because it is culturally uncomfortable for some. There are people out there who are confronted by the gruesomeness of the crucifixion. It is a graphic image after all. Does that mean in any way that we should limit the suffering that Christ had to endure for us? While some may argue that monocultural churches are simply one expression of church, the question proponents must answer is this: Does having a monoethnic community abandon key theological convictions in an attempt to be attractional? If people are troubled by diversity on earth, what are they going to do in heaven?

Third, monoethnic church advocates must be cautious not to be confused about the justification for multiethnic churches. For example, Steers explains:

> Some argue that since we are an increasingly multicultural society, our churches should become more multicultural. There is a certain logic to that. As long as there are people who want to be culturally and socially multicultural, or multiethnic, there also must be structures for them. Such ministries are crucial for healing America's racial and ethnic wounds. They potentially model the unbiased oneness that Jesus prayed for in John 17.[31]

This misrepresents the intent behind convictions about multiethnic ministry, which are not founded primarily out of a response to the changing face of society as Steers proposes. I do not dispute that the cultural mandate is important, and I appreciate its importance further in chapter 6. However, I believe that a multiethnic philosophy is mandated in the New Testament. Therefore, what we present here is not an idea that the multiethnic church is in some way a reaction to growing immigration; rather, it is what the Scriptures say on this issue. Yes, church planters and missiologists are widely welcoming the multiethnic church movement, but it is not because the culture is calling for it; it is because it is biblical. Mark DeYmaz articulates this point rather well: 'It is essential that the growing fascination with multiethnic church must be informed by sound theological reflection. In other words, the emerging movement must be based on biblical prescription rather than on current cultural description.'[32]

For this reason, this section is actually the most important part in the book because it presents the *why* behind multiethnic ministry. The latter part of this book focuses on the practical things, the *how* of multiethnic ministry. You may do none of the *how* stuff in this book, but I ask you to at least consider the *why*. Throughout these next chapters, I exhort you to test what I write and weigh it against what the Scriptures say. I pray that as you read, the Spirit of God will move in you to see the biblical mandate as clear cut in the Scriptures – although that part is up to God.

If you come to see the mandate as I do, then I ask that you take action. Of course, presenting biblical truths and asking people to take those truths on board is a very serious thing, especially if you get it wrong. All we can do is present the Scriptures as we read them, present Bible verses as they appear and trust that we are all reading the same thing. You be the judge.

CHAPTER 3
GOD'S VISION FOR THE ASYLUM

Seven hundred years before Christ, God publicly proclaimed his plan to create an asylum for all people groups: 'My house will be called a house of prayer for all nations' (Isa 56:7). All three Synoptic Gospels record Jesus publicly reaffirming his commitment to this vision. 'Is it not written: "My house will be called a house of prayer for all nations?"' (Mark 11:17; Matt 21:13; Luke 19:46).

    Given that Jesus himself endorsed this vision and, given its consistency with both the character and commission of God, proper theological reflection and application must be accorded to these passages. This 'all nations' vision should be the mandate that governs our churches on earth. Pastors and church leaders should be able to stand from the pulpit on a Sunday and evaluate the demographics of the church against God's vision.

One of the central themes in the book of Isaiah is the universal rule of God and the Father's plan for the restoration of a new heaven and new earth.[33] With such a focus on restoration, it shouldn't surprise us that at some point during the book's 66 chapters, God would communicate his grand plan for the future asylum. In fact, the message of Isaiah is so important that it commences with the declaration, 'Hear, O heavens, and listen, O earth; for the LORD has spoken ...' (Isa 1:2, NRSV). This is a message God wants the entire universe to hear and take notice of. Within the surrounding context, Isaiah 56:7 continues this theme of restoration by describing the characteristics of God's future sanctuary. God's asylum will be made up of people from all nationalities. It will literally be a house of prayer for all nations. As commentator Allan Harman writes, 'The gathering is going to be of Jew and Gentile together in God's Kingdom'.[34]

In a globalised world with international markets, the internet, social media and travel, the modern person can very easily speed-read such a text, overlooking just how remarkable a picture is being painted. However, to a seventh-century BC Jew, the picture being presented is something extraordinary. This statement would have been as shocking to an Israelite as Jesus' radical actions were when, quoting this passage, he entered the temple compound and overturned the money changers' tables. A seventh-century BC Israelite could not possibly have imagined a day when non-Jews would be able to enter the temple and worship God.

At the time of Jesus, although Jewish people were united under the religious traditions of their forefathers and shared their Old Testament Scriptures, different groups had emerged that held more nuanced positions of belief. Some of these groups, like the Pharisees and Sadducees, held influence, at times political; others, like the Essenes, sought to distance themselves from society. Nevertheless, for the most part, Israel saw itself as a nation set apart by God.

This unique calling was at times misrepresented. Through Israel's unique religion, laws and traditions, they were to be a blessing to the rest of the world and point people to the true God. Unfortunately, many abused this unique calling to esteem their own Jewish heritage, while holding negative attitudes about non-Jews. In fairness, sometimes these attitudes were held because of the immorality and idolatry displayed in the pagan nations that surrounded Israel. Not every Jewish person held such views, but this attitude was systemic in the culture and had an impact on religious devotion.

As a result of this attitude, Gentiles (that is, anyone not of Jewish descent) were forbidden from entering any further than the outer court of the temple compound. Even Jewish women were not given the same access to the temple precinct as men. The women had a compound of their own called the Court of the Women. This court was a little further in than that of the compound for non-Jews.

One of the morning prayers that has been preserved in Jewish literature contains the following blessing: 'Blessed are you O God, King of the Universe, Who has not made me ... a goy [Gentile] ... a slave ... and a woman'. This prayer comes centuries after Jesus, but the sentiment was there earlier. (Of course, such an attitude wasn't restricted to Jewish writers but is also found in Gentile writings). The prayer sounds very similar to a parable Jesus told about a self-righteous Pharisee (Luke 18:9–14): 'The Pharisee stood by himself and prayed: "God, I thank you that I am not like other people – robbers, evildoers, adulterers – or even like this tax collector"' (Luke 18:11).

None of this was God's intended purposes. In fact, it seems Paul was seeking to correct these very attitudes when he wrote: 'There is neither Jew nor Gentile, neither slave nor free, nor is there male and female, for you are all one in Christ Jesus' (Gal 3:28).

To a Jewish person, the temple compound was the holiest place on the planet. It became progressively holier the further inside you went. The most sacred point was an inner chamber known as the holy of holies. So sacred was this sanctuary that entry was only permissible by the high priest, once a year on the Day of Atonement, a day the Jews called Yom Kippur (Lev 16:2; Heb 9:7). According to popular legend, the high priest may have had a rope tied to his leg in the event that if he died inside, his body could be pulled out. The holy of holies was considered the place of the LORD's dwelling, literally his footstool.

After the first temple (Solomon's temple) was destroyed in 587–86 BC, a second temple was constructed by the returnees (Ezra 1:1–4; 2 Chron 36:22–23), which was eventually completed in 516 BC.[35] During the reign of the Roman client king, Herod the Great, a large-scale reconstruction project began around the year 20 BC to expand the temple mount. This expansion specifically included enclosing the outer court with colonnades as an area for the non-Jews known as the Court of the Gentiles. It was here that Jesus taught (Mark 14:49), healed (Matt 21:14), confronted religious officials (Matt 21:15) and drove out the merchants (Matt: 21:12; Mark 11:15; Luke 19:45).[36] Although Gentiles were permitted in the outer court, they were forbidden from entering anywhere near the inner courts. Warning signs were placed in both Greek and Latin, cautioning that the penalty for any breach of this law was death.[37] The Court of the Gentiles was basically a giant courtyard enclosed by colonnades, which operated as a marketplace or bazar of sorts. Travellers could buy souvenirs and sacrificial animals for religious piety and even change Roman coinage to a special coinage suitable for the temple tax.[38]

During the time of Jesus, Isaiah 56:7 was not something taken seriously by the Jews. It was the furthest thing from the mind of any self-respecting Jew. There's no way that a non-Jewish person was getting anywhere near the inner asylum of God. You could suggest that if anyone other than the God of Israel said the words of Isaiah 56:7, neither a seventh-century BC or a first-century AD Israelite would take it seriously. Consider what Isaiah was really asking a religiously and ethnically devout Jew to consider here: that one day in Yahweh's asylum, there would not only be Jews but Romans and Greeks and Egyptians and Samaritans and Babylonians and Assyrians and Ammonites and Moabites – all races. This is radical stuff.

Conservative estimates suggest that when Jesus overturned the money changers' tables, there may have been anywhere between 300,000 and 400,000 pilgrims in Jerusalem for the Passover celebrations.[39] When Christ walked into the temple compound, he saw all the buying and selling and the divisions between the Jews and the Gentiles and he drove them away. 'Is it not written: "My house will be called a house of prayer for all nations?" But you have made it "a den of robbers"' (Mark 11:17).

It is interesting that in this statement, Jesus combines two Old Testament references, citing both Isaiah 56:7, which we've looked at, and Jeremiah 7:11, which reads, 'Has this house, which bears my Name, become a den of robbers to you? But I have been watching! declares the LORD'.

Several hundred years after Jeremiah's time, Jesus arrives in the temple compound and gives proof that God has indeed been watching.

You've probably seen the familiar storyline on television where some parents are away, so their kids throw a party, invite their friends and end up trashing the house, only to have the parents return home early and survey the damage before clearing the house out. This is kind of what happens in this Gospel story. Jesus returns to his house and pronounces judgment over the corrupt activities taking place. He sees people being extorted at the money changers' tables. He sees people being exploited, having to pay exorbitant prices for animals to sacrifice for the

Passover. He also sees the way foreigners and Gentiles are being excluded from worship, and he isn't happy. Jesus accuses the Jewish people of failing to understand the words of Isaiah. They didn't understand the true purpose of God's house – to be a house of prayer for all people. Instead, they had perverted the system of true worship. Jesus was basically accusing the very people who thought they were serving God of being the real hindrance to the true vision.

God's care and concern for people from all ethnic backgrounds isn't something that begins in the New Testament. The Great Commission isn't just a once-off statement Jesus makes; there's a whole history behind it. Mission doesn't begin at Pentecost.[40] Yes, it takes on a whole new level of significance at that point, because the message we now carry is one of eternal reconciliation with God. But God was still very much concerned for the nations in the Old Testament. After all, the Psalmist declared, 'All the nations you have made will come and worship before you, LORD; they will bring glory to your name' (Ps 86:9). Sometimes Christians mistakenly think that the New Testament is all that matters and fail to consider how God's salvation plan was unfolding in the Old Testament. We see very clearly God's love for all people in the Old Testament and how he wanted to use Israel.

I've already mentioned the great promises made to Abraham, that through him God would bless people from all nations. But we see some other great indications of God's mandate to reach the nations throughout the Old Testament. In the book of Exodus, we learn that God didn't just free Israelites. Rather, a 'mixed multitude also went up with them, along with flocks and herds, a very large number of livestock' (Exod 12:38). Historically, we know that Egypt enslaved people from a number of conquered nations.[41] Therefore, God was happy to not only redeem the nation of Israel but also to liberate others. We can find other examples of this. During the conquests of Joshua, we see Rahab, a Canaanite prostitute, spared along with her family and integrated into the people of God. She boldly declared,

> 'I know that the LORD has given you this land and that a great fear of you has fallen on us, so that all who live in this country are melting in fear because of you. We have heard how the LORD dried up the water of the Red Sea for you when you came out of Egypt, and what you did to Sihon and Og, the two kings of the Amorites east of the Jordan, whom you completely destroyed. When we heard of it, our hearts melted in fear and everyone's courage failed because of you, for the LORD your God is God in heaven above and on the earth below ...' (Josh 2:8–11).

This was a fundamental purpose for the nation of Israel. Through Israel's unique law, unique lifestyle and holiness, the nations would flock to them and declare the same thing Rahab did. Deuteronomy says,

> Observe them carefully, for this will show your wisdom and understanding to the nations, who will

> hear about all these decrees and say, 'Surely this great nation is a wise and understanding people'. What other nation is so great as to have their gods near them the way the LORD our God is near us whenever we pray to him? And what other nation is so great as to have such righteous decrees and laws as this body of laws I am setting before you today? (Deut 4:6–8).

We see this lived out in a practical way after the fall of Jericho and Ai, during the covenant renewal, where even foreigners are integrated into Israel's spiritual family.

> All the Israelites, with their elders, officials and judges, were standing on both sides of the ark of the covenant of the LORD, facing the Levitical priests who carried it. Both the foreigners living among them and the native-born were there. Half of the people stood in front of Mount Gerizim and half of them in front of Mount Ebal, as Moses the servant of the LORD had formerly commanded when he gave instructions to bless the people of Israel (Josh 8:33).

Israel's geographic placement made it ideal for this scenario, given that throughout its history Israel found itself situated between some great superpowers like Egypt, Assyria, Babylon, Persia, Greece and Rome. Their very location served God's purpose.

Israel may have done a miserable job at living up to God's standard, but nonetheless we see a few more glimpses throughout the Old Testament.

During the time of the Judges, we see Naomi, the daughter-in-law of Ruth, marry Boaz and become integrated into the covenant people of God. She, a foreign woman, declared to Ruth, 'Where you go I will go, and where you stay I will stay. Your people will be my people and your God my God' (Ruth 1:16).

In 1 Kings, the Queen of Sheba, having heard of Solomon's fame and the special relationship he had with the LORD, proclaimed:

> 'The report I heard in my own country about your achievements and your wisdom is true. But I did not believe these things until I came and saw with my own eyes. Indeed, not even half was told me; in wisdom and wealth you have far exceeded the report I heard. How happy your people must be! How happy your officials, who continually stand before you and hear your wisdom! Praise be to the LORD your God, who has delighted in you and placed you on the throne of Israel. Because of the LORD's eternal love for Israel, he has made you king to maintain justice and righteousness' (1 Kgs 10:6–9).

In 2 Kings, God used Elisha to cure Naaman, a commander from a foreign army, of leprosy. After his healing, Naaman declares, 'Now I know that there is no God in all the world except in Israel ...' (2 Kgs 5:15).

God's care for the nation is an especially prevalent theme throughout the Prophets. Not only do we have Jonah, a prophet whose entire mission was directed at preaching repentance to a foreign nation, but the entire message of the prophetic literature has as an integral theme the idea that God is going to do something great with the nations. Where Israel failed to gather the nations, God, the true ruler of the heavens and the earth, will:

> 'My name will be great among the nations, from where the sun rises to where it sets. In every place incense and pure offerings will be brought to me, because my name will be great among the nations,' says the LORD Almighty (Mal 1:11).

Similarly, Isaiah foresaw a beautiful day when the nations will return to God, even those nations that were synonymous with Israel's oppression, such as Egypt and Assyria.

> In that day there will be a highway from Egypt to Assyria. The Assyrians will go to Egypt and the Egyptians to Assyria. The Egyptians and Assyrians will worship together (Isa 19:23).

What a powerful image of reconciliation: the nations coming together to worship the one true God!

If the clear vision communicated by God, and by Christ, is for churches to be multiethnic, why do we still have large numbers of churches choosing to ignore this mandate in search of establishing monoethnic churches? The reason is simple. In the words of that ancient Platonic proverb, 'birds of a feather flock together'. Most monoethnic churches are created with the intention of reaching one particular nationality, because the process of growing the church is much easier. Many churches in Australia are products of the huge waves of immigration that have been prevalent throughout Australian history. When large numbers of people move to a country, it makes sense to set up churches filled with people from similar cultural backgrounds. The problem is that, while you might give those migrants a solid support system and a community to feel a part of, the thinking is short-term. In the long run, in everyday life, those same individuals are mixing with people of different ethnicities. They are learning the native language to obtain employment and integrating into wider society. They are also having children who need to form their own identity.

My fear is that many churches today find themselves strategically situated in some remarkable multiethnic communities, much like Israel was situated strategically among the nations, yet fail to reach out to such people and thus fail to embody God's vision. It is our responsibility to make sure that we are doing our utmost to aspire towards Jesus' vision for a church that is a house of prayer *for all people*. Otherwise we risk inadvertently doing the same thing the Jewish people of Jesus' day were doing – stifling God's vision. It is true this side of eternity that no church will be perfect, and we're certainly not saying that if Jesus came to our church today, he'd be driving people away. What we *are* saying is that the church is meant to be multiethnic.

It is a great tragedy when you walk into a church that has a heart for God but at the same time has a 'Court of the Gentiles'. Some may argue that this is the most effective way to do ministry in their cultural context. They might also say that all they're trying to do is remove cultural barriers to conversion and not force people to have to assimilate into an unfamiliar community. But God's vision does away with all cultural barriers. God's vision for the church is not bound by our own understandings. God's purposes far exceed our own. God's church is a supernatural community that defies our natural inclinations and boundary markers. When people accept Christ, they must embrace Christ's all-encompassing vision. This is part of what it means to become a citizen of God's kingdom. The values of God's kingdom often challenge our existing paradigms for what we believe the church to be. God does this through the transforming of our minds and thought patterns, through his word and Holy Spirit. God's vision is for a multiethnic asylum, and we too must take this ideal seriously, even when it challenges our existing models.

CHAPTER 4
THE EARLY CHURCH ASYLUM

One lens through which the book of Acts might be viewed is as a manual defending the multiethnic mandate. As the sequel to his Gospel, Luke is very deliberate in highlighting the way the Holy Spirit emerges as the primary driver and continuer of Christ's mission in the world, through the church.[42] The book of Acts is a collection of stories affirming how God began fulfilling his great commission in the actual reality of historical events. As such, modern readers need to pay very close attention to the (for want of a better word) shape and demographics of the early church.

Acts begins with the disciples in Jerusalem waiting for the Spirit to equip them for the Commission to reach the nations (Acts 1:1–8). The key verse in understanding Luke's purpose is Acts 1:8:[43] 'But you will receive power when the Holy Spirit comes on you; and you will be my witnesses in Jerusalem, and in all Judea and Samaria, and to the end of the earth'.

We know from this that the remainder of Luke's account is about articulating how it is that the gospel goes from Jerusalem to Judea and Samaria and then to the end of the earth. In other words, it is about how Christianity became a multiethnic movement! Luke, a companion of Paul, no doubt understood Paul's frustration over the Jew and Gentile issue. In Acts, therefore, it seems that Luke wished to celebrate the expansion of the gospel to all nations and in the process, make it very clear that God's mission is indeed multiethnic.

The timeline of Acts is deliberately arranged with this purpose in mind:

- Luke begins at Pentecost, where the church is equipped to reach the nations. (1–2:41)

- The early chapters are devoted to telling the story of the success of the gospel in Jerusalem (2:42—8:1).

- By chapter 8, Luke starts sharing how the gospel went beyond Jerusalem. He begins with the persecution that scattered the church throughout Judea and Samaria (8:1–3).

- This is followed by the story of how Philip takes the gospel throughout Judea and Samaria (8:4–25), then by the conversion of an Ethiopian eunuch (8:26–40).

- After this comes the story of Paul and how one of the greatest advocates of all time for a multiethnic church became a follower of Jesus (chapter 9).

- Next, Peter is challenged by God, during his encounter with Cornelius, to adopt a multiethnic framework (chapter 10). Peter reassures everyone that God's vision for a multiethnic church is authentic, and his audience is in turn convinced when they find out that the Gentiles have also received the Spirit. The receiving of the Spirit was a clear sign that the Gentiles had also been invited to be a part of Jesus' house of prayer (Acts 11:1–18).

- Subsequently, Luke describes an example of evangelists who were getting it right and preaching to both Jews and Gentiles, and we are told that the hand of the Lord was with them. This is the beginning of the church in Antioch, the first multiethnic church (11:19–30).

- From Antioch, the believers were called to go out to the rest of the Mediterranean and Asia Minor (Acts 13–14). As Paul declared: ' … for this is what the Lord has commanded us: "I have made you a light for the Gentiles, that you may bring salvation to the ends of the earth"' (Acts 13:47). The response? 'When the Gentiles heard this, they were glad and honoured the word of the Lord; and all who were appointed for eternal life believed' (Acts 13:48).

- Lastly, some of the issues hindering the movements advancement were dealt with during the Council of Jerusalem (Acts 15). This paved the way for Paul, as documented in the remainder of Acts, to go throughout the empire, preaching the gospel in Galatia, Macedonia, (Philippi), Thessalonica, Corinth, Ephesus, Athens, Rome ...

Today, the book of Acts continues. It is being written in the lives of millions of believers from across the globe who are turning to receive Jesus.

ANTIOCH AS A MODEL

When the subject of multiethnic ministry comes up, I find that hesitancies often arise with relation to the practicalities. There are many legitimate questions that need answering. As a mission strategy, it is certainly easier to nurture a church that caters to people from common demographics. However, just because it is easier doesn't mean it is biblical.

The Bible not only communicates the vision for a multiethnic asylum, it also goes one step further by providing a practical example of such a church. This asylum was the church in Antioch. Although Jerusalem was the epicentre from which Christianity exploded, Antioch should be regarded as the prototypical church for modern churches to replicate. Today, it is popular to closely examine the model followed by the church in Jerusalem and overlook the significance of Antioch.

The church at Antioch was one of five major churches during the first thousand years of Christianity. After Christianity officially became the state religion of the Roman Empire, Antioch formally became recognised along with the churches at Rome, Jerusalem, Alexandria and Constantinople as one the five main episcopal sees dividing the administration of Christianity. The community of believers developed in Antioch after a wave of persecution forced Christians to flee Jerusalem (Acts 8:4; 11:19–21). The believers travelled north along the coastline of the Mediterranean through modern day Lebanon, preaching the gospel in townships in Cyprus, Tyre, Sidon and Ptolemais. Finally, they reached Antioch, three-hundred miles north of Jerusalem, in the southern part of modern-day Turkey, close to the Syrian border. Along the Orontes River, Antioch was the third largest city of the Roman Empire, behind Rome and Alexandria. Estimates have varied for the size of Antioch's population from 100,000 to anywhere upwards of 600,000.[44] However, the accepted estimates during the time of the book of Acts are around 300,000.[45]

Antioch had an interesting history that paved the way for Christianity to take off in the dramatic fashion it did. The city was founded around 300 BC by Seleucus I Nicator, one of Alexander the Great's generals. Like several other cities (for example, Antioch Pisidia in Acts 13:14–52), he named it after his father Antiochus. The city was wealthy and cosmopolitan; its geographic, military and economic location made it a gateway between Asia and the Mediterranean, with close links to the trade routes and rich natural resources.[46] The city was always home to a diverse range of people, with a mixed population of local Syrians, Greeks, Macedonians and Jews. Furthermore, when the Roman Empire formally conquered Antioch under Pompey in 64 BC, it became the capital of the Syrian province, becoming home to many Romans as well.[47] Antioch's Jewish population numbered anywhere from 25,000–60,000. Many were wealthy and enjoyed the benefits of being part of a political state, with exemption from military service and permission to practise religious piety in their own tradition.[48]

Consequently, when the Apostle Paul arrived in approximately 43 AD (almost 100 years after Julius Caesar visited the city), Antioch was under a period of profound rebuilding.[49] This made it fertile ground for Christianity's first multiethnic church. Fascinatingly, Antioch was a city where religious and cultural barriers were crossed, even before the emergence of Christianity.[50] Josephus records that Jewish synagogues were 'constantly attracting to their religious ceremonies multitudes of Greeks'.[51] Perhaps these were the God-fearing Greeks that the Bible talks about, who were attracted to monotheism (Acts 10:22; 13:16, 26, 43; 16:14; 17:4; 18:7). One of these may have been a man by the name of Nicolaus, who converted and was appointed by the church as one of the Hellenistic leaders (Acts 6:5).[52] Naturally, when the earliest messengers came to Antioch (Acts 11:29–21), this new philosophy would have sparked the interest of the Hellenised people.

Unfortunately, despite the believer's zeal, they lacked one thing – consistency. Luke records unequivocally that they only preached the gospel among the Jews (Acts 11:19).

Immediately, warning bells should be ringing in the minds of all church leaders when reading this. We must caution ourselves from only preaching the gospel to certain types of people. If Luke was to document the Acts of the modern church, would he say that your church went across the suburbs preaching the gospel only to Indian people, or Chinese people, Filipino people, Korean people, Greek people, Anglo-Celtic people? Yet when Jesus said go and make disciples of *all* nations, Jesus also said, 'you will be my witnesses in Jerusalem, and in all Judea and Samaria, and to the ends of the earth'. Ministering to people from only one ethnic background is like ministering in Jerusalem only. As we move beyond our own nationalities, we move to Judea or Samaria – and eventually the ends of the earth.

For further reflection, I want to take a brief detour from Antioch to look at the High Priestly Prayer of Jesus in John 17. I draw here on the work of Mark DeYmaz, who devotes detailed attention to the various components of Jesus' prayer and how they can be used to advance the argument for multiethnic churches.[53] Mark helpfully recognises that Jesus prays that his followers (both the disciples before him and those to come) will be 'one' (John 17:21–23):

> Christ prayed specifically that future generations of believers would be one so that the world would know God's love and believe. In this way and by

> this means, Christ stated his mission would be accomplished through others and, ultimately, his Father glorified. What Jesus intends for us (the local church), then, is clear: we have been called to be one for the sake of the gospel ... Indeed, when men and women of diverse backgrounds walk together as one in Christ, they uniquely reflect the Father's love on earth as it is in heaven. More than that, their oneness of mind, love, spirit, and purpose proclaim the gospel in a most powerful and compelling way.[54]

Only by being unified can the church fulfil its purpose to take the gospel to all nations.

To advance this further, Jesus prayed to his Father concerning the disciples, 'As you have sent me into the world, so I have sent them into the world' (John 17:18). Can you and I truly be sent into the world, as Jesus was sent into the world, if we feel that we are only sent to one people group? Mission experts today use a concept known as *missio Dei* to describe our 'sentness' into the world.[55] Although complex, the central idea is that God is, by nature, a sending God or a 'missionary God'.[56] David Bosch argues that mission is something intrinsic to God's nature, calling it an 'attribute of God'.[57] Its formulation is grounded in the doctrine of the Trinity.[58] The common description is that God, through a series of sending acts, sent his Son into the world. After Jesus' mission was complete, together the Father and Son sent the Spirit as our Comforter to live with those who believe and empower us for mission. Collectively, the Godhead sends the church to be God's representative to the world (Matt 28:19; John 20:21–22; 14:26; 17:18; Luke 24:49; Acts 1:4).[59] It is essential to recognise the centrality of the theme of mission in Scripture, because it describes God's activity in history.[60] In the Old Testament, God sent prophets, the law, judges and kings to lead people. In the New Testament, the Triune God sends the church into the world. 'In the last days, God says, "I will pour out my Spirit on all people …"' (Acts 2:17).

Returning to Antioch, Luke goes on to record the actions of a select few. These select few who as they went about their daily business, recognised that the city of Antioch had a large proportion of Gentiles (Acts 11:20–21). Subsequently as they went about their daily business, they preached the good news to non-Jews as well as Jews. 'Some of them, however, men from Cyprus and Cyrene, went to Antioch and began to speak to Greeks also, telling them the good news about the LORD Jesus' (Acts 11:20).

Notice the word 'also' in this verse. The Greek word here is the conjunction *kai* (translated as 'and' or 'also') and is unbelievably important.[61] Why? Because it wasn't just that these believers realised no one was preaching to the Greeks and decided to set up a church exclusively for them. Instead, they incorporated them as part of their wider evangelism strategies. Remember, Antioch was full of non-Jews. If the population of Jews was only 25,000 and the entire population of Antioch was over 300,000, it wouldn't make sense to restrict sharing the good news to less than 8.5 per cent of the population. This is a practical example of a heterogeneous mission strategy from Scripture itself. These unnamed evangelists, who were not Apostles, changed the face of Christianity. Had God not inspired and transformed the hearts of these evangelists, Christianity would look very different today. There would be no multiethnic asylum; you and I may not have heard the gospel.

Additionally, it is recorded that the Lord's hand was with them (Acts 11:21). In other words, this strategy is God-approved. Although Luke records on several occasions that a great number came to faith as a result of the apostles' preaching (Acts 2:41, 47; 4:4; 11:24), nowhere else does he reference the hand of the Lord. As you can see, the believers at Antioch weren't practising a homogenous unit principle style of evangelism. Instead, the church in Antioch was practising the heterogeneous unit principle.

John Stott commented on the importance of this, saying, 'The addition ... of "also" [*kai*] is important. It is not that the evangelisation of the Jews must stop, but that the evangelisation of the Gentiles must begin'.[62]

Antioch would have been a remarkable church; nowhere else in the ancient world could you find a group of Jews and Gentiles worshipping God together. Perhaps even more extraordinary was that this group of Jews and Gentiles owed their allegiance to a God who was crucified. Their Messiah was not a political ruler, as the Jews expected. Their Deity was not one among many, as the pagans worshipped, nor was their Lord a delusional Caesar who thought he was king of the universe.

Their sovereign king was universal ruler of both Jew and Gentile, their LORD was LORD of all – their Messiah was Immanuel, their Christ was crucified and raised to life.

The story of Antioch gets even more remarkable. From its humble beginnings, we learn that Barnabas was sent to Antioch (Acts 11:22–24). After seeing a flourishing community, he travelled west to Tarsus to inform Paul. Afterwards, both Paul and Barnabas spent a year serving this thriving church (11:25–26). Here we have Paul, a Jew from Tarsus with Roman citizenship, ministering alongside Barnabas, a Levite from Cyprus. Hereafter, Antioch was not only a multiethnic church but also had a diverse leadership team.

Antioch then becomes the launching pad for the spread of Christianity throughout the Gentile world (Acts 13:3; 15:22–36; 18:22–23).[63] From Antioch, the disciples take the gospel through many of the illustrious New Testament communities we learn about today: Philippi, Thessalonica, Athens, Corinth, Ephesus and Rome. And despite all of the controversy in the early New Testament church relating to the integration of Gentiles into the church, Antioch will always be remembered as the place where something extraordinary happened. It was at the church in Antioch where the term 'Christians' was first used to describe a group of followers of Christ (Acts 11:23–26). 'So for a whole year Barnabas and Saul met with the church and taught great numbers of people. The disciples were called Christians first at Antioch' (Acts 11:26).

This term is now the universal term that we use to describe any follower of Jesus, be they Jew, Gentile, Protestant, Catholic, man, woman or child. This fact may seem to some like just a useful piece of biblical trivia, but it is significant that the term was first employed to describe the community in Antioch. The meaning of names is very important in Scripture. Take Jesus, meaning 'the LORD saves', or Israel, meaning 'wrestles with God'. We cannot merely think that the name 'Christian' today is trivial. There was something about the way that Antioch Christians did church that others had not seen before. This prompted the use of new language to describe the community.

Prior to this time, the Christian movement had been rooted within the context of Judaism and was therefore under its banner. Within the early New Testament church, the believers were frequently referred to as the 'saints' (9:13), 'brothers' (1:16 9:30) or 'disciples' (6.1), 'believers' (10:45) or 'saved' (2:47). However, by the second century, the term Christian had become the enduring name.[64] The name was likely accorded to the community of believers in Antioch from those ordinary Antiochene citizens looking in from the outside (Acts 26:28; 1 Pet 4:16). There can be no question from the historical data available to us that by the late 40s AD, Christians were starting to be identified separately from traditional Orthodox Jews, at least by the general populace. The term may have originally been used as an insult, but it was adopted as a badge of honour by the church.

This raises an interesting question: why was Antioch so special as to be the first place where Christians could be associated with such a term? Why wasn't the term first used in association with the church in Jerusalem? After all, Jerusalem was the most profound place within the ministry of Jesus, as the location of his death and resurrection; what's more, the gospel message went out from Jerusalem. This was also the place where the Holy Spirit first came upon the believers in the upper room (Act 2) and where the church numerically exploded from hundreds to thousands of converts as the Apostles preached with conviction and performed many miracles. Should not the use of such a term as 'Christian' have begun in Jerusalem?

The only logical conclusion is that first century semanticists needed a new term to describe this new group of people. Contextually, the term simply denoted those followers or associates of the one called 'Christ', much like the Herodians and Herod in Mark 3:6 and 12:13.[65] Yet it was the inclusion of a large number of Gentiles into the church at Antioch that seems to have been the catalyst for a new term demarcating this distinct group of people. The people of Antioch looked for a way to describe this new movement which had attracted both Jews and non-Jews in droves. No such terminology yet existed in any lexicon, so they invented one after the movement's originator.

The fact that the term was first used in Antioch is further evidence that a church seeking to minister to only one ethnic group is misapplying church growth models and the homogenous unit principle. Against the backdrop of Acts and the New Testament church, the monoethnic approach crumbles.

Furthermore, when we read between the lines of Scripture, we recognise that a lot of the issues the New Testament church faced were the inevitable questions that naturally arose as Jews and Gentiles started fellowshipping together. Questions about circumcision, the law, the Council of Jerusalem, dietary requirements and table fellowship were all examples of how the early church sought to emerge from its Jewish foundations. These questions, although they were rooted in centuries of ethnocentric attitudes, required pastoral responses. A monoethnic community wouldn't need answers to such questions. For instance, concerning the question of circumcision, Jewish believers wouldn't need to ask Paul his thoughts on the matter, unless Gentiles were entering the church.

Finally, even the common first-century Christian greeting of 'grace and peace' has multiethnicity written all over it. The word grace comes from the common Greek greeting *charis*[66] and peace (the Greek *eirenee*) had the Hebrew concept of shalom (Num 6:24–26; Judg 6:22–23; Isa 57:19; Ps 29:11; 1 Chron 12:18; Ezra 5:7; Luke 24:36; John 20:19).[67] The combination was a customary greeting in early Christian circles (Rom 1:7; 1 Cor 1:3; 2 Cor 1:2; Gal 1:3; Eph 1:2; Phil 1:2; Col 1:2; 1 Thess 1:1; 2 Thess 1:2; 1 Tim 1:2; 2 Tim 1:2; Titus 1:4; Phlm 1:3; 1 Pet 1:2; 2 Pet 1:2; 2 John 1:3; Rev 1:4).[68] This greeting incorporated the very diversity in Christ that made the early church multiethnic.

The influence of the church in Antioch should not be understated. Because of what God did in Antioch, Christianity could never adhere to a pattern of conformity among the cultural groups. Never can anyone hear the word Christian and mentally construct a description of what a Christian should look like. They can never say that a Christian has blonde hair, blues eyes, or fair skin and dark hair. We can say honestly that without Antioch, there would have been no Parkside Church.

There is one more important aspect to be explored. So far, our asylum seeker vessel has voyaged past God's vision for a multiethnic asylum as well as its practical expression found in the early church at Antioch. Now we must set a course for our final destination as we navigate the waters of what the future and final asylum will look like. Our place of disembarkment will be the great heavenly multiethnic asylum that awaits all those on board our vessel.

CHAPTER 5
THE FUTURE ASYLUM

I would like the reader to imagine where this is all heading.

> After this I looked, and there before me was a great multitude that no one could count, from every nation, tribe, people and language, standing before the throne and before the Lamb. They were wearing white robes and were holding palm branches in their hands (Rev 7:9).

Every sermon you hear, every time you evangelise, every person you care for, every cent you invest in God's work – the entire mission of the church – comes down to this one eternal vision, when a great multitude from across the globe will one day worship before the throne of God!

The Book of Revelation is apocalyptic literature.[69] Here we are given an eschatological glimpse into where everything is heading and what the church of Christ will look like for all eternity.[70] The book of Revelation is like a movie maker who shows the audience a glimpse of the end scene of a movie at the start. This scene is a flash forward to a point towards which the main characters are moving. It doesn't unveil everything, but it shows enough to help us understand that the rest of the movie is progressing to that point. Revelation captures the contemporary images and world context that the earliest Christians were living in, while giving them a greater narrative of what was to come.

Revelation unequivocally and unapologetically supports the notion that the heavenly church, in all its restored glory, will be multiethnic. That is an undeniable fact. No theologian or Christian can argue otherwise. There will be no separate monoethnic congregations in heaven. It will be one community of God's people worshipping together before God, alongside the angels, for all eternity. That is God's ultimate asylum, and we eagerly await this future hope. God's purposes come to their glorious fulfillment as humans from every tongue, nation and tribe gather together, forming one magnificent asylum. Therefore, as a post-resurrection community, it is our responsibility to model such a community on earth as it is in heaven.

Since the time Jesus first instructed us to reach the nations, the church has been sailing towards the great asylum described in Revelation 7:9. This verse is crucial to the way the church understands its mission in the world. As already explored, statements like those found in Isaiah 56:7 and Mark 11:17 represent Christ's vision for his church and the Great Commission is his way of achieving that vision. Accordingly, Revelation 7:9 paints a picture of a day when Christ's vision will come to fruition. It is there so that we can know and picture what the future holds. If Jesus didn't want us to learn something from what the end will look like, why bother revealing it to John in the first place? For you and I can't achieve a vision unless we can perceive what the end result will look like. An Olympic sprinter cannot win a gold medal unless he or she knows what they ultimately wish to achieve. As you probably know by now, if we believe that the many authors of the different books of the Bible were under the divine inspiration of the Holy Spirit, then it stands to reason that everything in the Bible is included for a purpose. There is nothing in its pages by mistake.

What can the church learn from Revelation 7:9? How can we better apply its meaning and model the diversity it teaches? When people walk into our church on a Sunday, do they get a glimpse of what God's vision for the church entails? People must see tangible evidence that people from every nation, tribe and tongue are being united as one body in Christ.

A crucial detail of the text is that the great multitude drawn from every nation, tribe, people and language is innumerable. It is important for modern readers to keep in mind that the earliest Christians didn't worship in a megachurch, with another megachurch down the road. They worshipped in house churches and were a small, often persecuted, minority of the Roman

Empire. Therefore, it would have been unfathomable to imagine a day when their numbers would be incalculable,[71] with no Roman census, like that at the time of Jesus' birth, able to count them. This whole picture fulfils God's promise to Abraham: 'I will multiply your descendants as the stars of heaven, and will give your descendants all these lands; and by your descendants all the nations of the earth shall be blessed' (Gen 26:4; see also Gen 17:4 and Gal 3:8).[72] It is this multitude that has been purchased with the blood of Jesus on the cross:[73] 'And they sang a new song, saying: "You are worthy to take the scroll and to open its seals, because you were slain, and with your blood you purchased for God persons from every tribe and language and people and nation" (Rev 5:9). This 'church for all nations' slogan is found repeatedly throughout the book in a variety of forms (Rev 5:9; 10:11; 11:9; 13:7; 14:6; 17:15; 21:24, 26). Commentator Grant Osborn affirms that this repetition is not there by mistake. It stresses God's universal mission to reach people from every nation. It brings together all of salvation history.[74]

Interestingly, the Greek word for nations, *ethnos* (*goy* in the Hebrew) – from which we get our contemporary word, ethnic – often carried negative connotations in biblical times, as it sometimes does today. Although the term is neutral, it comes with a lot of baggage. To a devout Jew in the ancient world, it meant someone who was pagan and from a Gentile nation. In the more culturally sophisticated circles, it referred to someone considered a heathen. Similarly, the term 'ethnic' can convey negative images. Every society is beset with its own examples of discrimination and oppression towards the people they have rejected due to ethnicity. When we think about the horrific examples of 'ethnic cleansing' littered throughout history, we see sin in one of its most destructive forms. Whether we are talking about the Holocaust, the Armenian genocide or the Bosnian genocide, the list is lengthy and has resulted in many atrocities and much loss of life. While such examples each have their own contributing geopolitical contexts, they all commence with the notion that some ethnicities are inferior to others.

Even at a personal level, we must test our own prejudices and phobias towards people of different ethnicities. While we may be dismayed by large-scale ethnic cleansing, we all need to reflect on the subtle ways we can look down on others, whether it takes the form of racial joking or the instinctive ways we prejudge others and give preference to those from our own ethnic background. We can deceive ourselves by failing to recognise discrimination when it is present in our own hearts. Nevertheless, here in the book of Revelation, as in other key biblical texts, the terminology is used in the most positive light (see Isa 11:10 and 66:18–21). Historian Craig Keener says this:

> The international focus of Revelation goes far beyond its contemporaries' expectations and proves central to the New Testament teaching because it is so radical: Gentile Christians can be grafted into God's people ... Yet the gospel challenges our prejudices ... We have no right to decide who will receive God's good news, and we may be grateful

that those who witnessed to us or to our spiritual predecessors did not prejudge its proper recipients. *But if we claim any loyalty to Christ's gospel, this requires us to transcend our cultural prejudices both to witness to and to lovingly embrace believers from all cultures.*[75] (emphasis mine)

REVERSAL OF BABEL

Revelation 7:9 marks a reversal of the Babel curse. In the famous story from Genesis 10, as a direct consequence of human sin, humankind becomes separated by language. This action has resulted in the racial, national and cultural barriers we still experience today. However, the new creation will no longer be separated by the consequences of the fall. Revelation 7:9 is a promise that God as part of his new creation has reinstated humanity to its pre-fall capacities. In God's asylum, our ethnicities with not be a source of division. Instead, the gathering together of all nations will be a visible expression that God's redemptive plans are complete.

We are often very good at describing what the new creation will look like. We know that in the kingdom of God there are no poor; neither is there sickness, disease, famine or death. There will be no miscommunications, no threat of nuclear weapons or need to bear arms. There will be no natural disasters and no global warming. There will be no political tension, ethnic persecution, no dictators, tyrants or despots, no wars, fascism or need for international organisations like the United Nations. The kingdom of God is *the* United Nation.

I fear, however, that the notion of 'every nation, tribe and tongue' is often left out of descriptions of this new creation. Perhaps the reason is that we are accustomed to looking at an atlas. When we stare at that atlas, we notice it has borders and lines that mark out different countries and people groups. Therefore, to imagine a world without borders, governments and militaries is completely foreign to us. However, the Bible calls us to perceive a new world in which the reign of God is supreme over all people. In contrast to the times of the Tower of Babel, when the languages divided humanity, the book of Revelation paints a remarkable reversal and celebration of different nationalities worshipping God. No longer will the establishment of different nationalities and dialects be a curse upon the earth. This will not devalue the existing connections people have to their cultural heritage. Instead it will bring to completion God's intended purposes. Revelation 7:9 is a celebration of God's power to unite people from every nation, tribe and tongue under his rule.

GOING DEEPER

Hints of the visionary experience described in Revelation 7:9 can be found elsewhere in Scripture.

> In my vision at night I looked, and there before me was one like a son of man, coming with the clouds of heaven. He approached the Ancient of Days and

was led into his presence. He was given authority, glory and sovereign power; all nations and peoples of every language worshiped him. His dominion is an everlasting dominion that will not pass away, and his kingdom is one that will never be destroyed (Dan 7:13–14).

In your relationships with one another, have the same mindset as Christ Jesus: Who, being in very nature God, did not consider equality with God something to be used to his own advantage rather, he made himself nothing by taking the very nature of a servant, being made in human likeness. And being found in appearance as a man, he humbled himself by becoming obedient to death – even death on a cross! Therefore, God exalted him to the highest place and gave him the name that is above every name, that at the name of Jesus every knee should bow, in heaven and on earth and under the earth, and every tongue acknowledge that Jesus Christ is LORD, to the glory of God the Father (Phil 2:5–11).[76]

These are fascinating pieces of Scripture. Scholars have spent years writing books and exegetically examining individual words found in both of these passages. They contain all sorts of questions about theological concepts such as the incarnation of Jesus, the Trinity and the Son of Man. Nonetheless, what is not ambiguous is the extent of sovereignty in Daniel's description of this Son of Man and Paul's description of Jesus in Philippians exercise. In both references, the Son of Man receives something only God is worthy to receive: worship and dominion over all nations. Both passages, along with Revelation 7:9, emphasise the futuristic and universal worship Jesus will receive.

Nations, peoples and languages are apparent in all three passages. In the book of Daniel, the key theme is that God, not the pagan ruling dynasties of Babylon and Persia, is the sovereign ruler over all the nations. And, as Daniel 7 depicts, there will be a time when the universal reign of God will be manifested in the flesh and all will submit to the lordship of the Son of Man, who has received all authority from the Ancient of Days (a title for God). After his resurrection, Jesus boldly pronounced, 'All authority in heaven and on earth has been given to me' (Matt 28:18). Jesus certainly identified himself as the Son of Man from Daniel 7.

Likewise, in the letter to the Philippians, one of Paul's central themes is our heavenly citizenship (Phil 3:7). The church in Philippi was not your normal church. Contrary to the traditional Jewish mantra, it was established by Paul and a group of women (see Acts 16:11–15). The church was undergoing strong persecution from the empire, and amid this Paul reminds them to stay unified and appeals to the model for humility set by Jesus himself. This Christ-hymn reminds the church not just of Jesus' incredible sacrifice but the way that he has been exalted to the point that everyone in heaven and earth reports to him. As in Daniel 7 and Revelation 7:9, Paul foresaw a future day where people from all nations would see Jesus in the flesh and bow down to his authority. The phrasing found in Philippians is a reflection on Isaiah 45:22–23:

> Turn to me and be saved,
> all you ends of the earth;
> for I am God, and there is no other.
> By myself I have sworn,
> my mouth has uttered in all integrity
> a word that will not be revoked:
> Before me every knee will bow;
> by me every tongue will swear.

The Greek word *glóssa*, found in Revelation 7:9 and translated as either 'language' or 'tongue', is found also in Philippians 2:11. Accordingly, perhaps when Paul states that every tongue will acknowledge that Jesus Christ is LORD, he's not just saying that individuals will make a formal declaration with their mouths that Jesus is LORD, but that this testimony will ring out in many different languages. This sort of declaration was incredibly dangerous to the first readers. There's a reason why people like Daniel and members of the early church were persecuted. The message that 'Jesus is LORD' was extremely confrontational. In effect, they were saying, the Babylonians don't have sovereignty, the Romans don't rule the world – instead it is Jesus Christ, the Son of Man, who has all authority in heaven and earth. It is to Jesus alone – not Nebuchadnezzar, not Caesar – that all nations will worship and pay homage to. Daniel, Paul and John were convinced that their God was the God of the nations.

A PAULINE-FLAVOURED ARGUMENT: 'WHAT'S WRONG WITH A PATCHWORK QUILT?'

If our Scriptures clearly communicate God's mission is for our churches to be inclusive of people from all nations, how can some of us justify limiting our mission to making disciples of one nation?

But, we can argue, it makes practical sense to reach people of similar ethnicity. That way we are not overcome by language, cultural or worldview barriers.

What then of the unbeliever who comes into the church and does not fit the demographics and yet seeks fellowship? Are we to drive them away?

Well, one could argue, there are plenty of other churches where they will feel more comfortable. It is like a restaurant; some people like Indian food, others like Hispanic food, still others like Chinese or Lebanese food. And we don't have multiethnic restaurants, do we?

Are we then to conclude that the church of God is divided? Is the body of Christ divided based on nationality or ethnicity?

Of course not! Christ is not divided. We just appreciate that God calls different people to reach specific nationalities. There's nothing wrong with our churches modelling that. Some he calls to be missionaries to the Asians; others he calls to minister among the Africans.

So then, shall we determine that Jesus gave us all a different command? Did he not instruct us to reach all people as part of the same commission?

Yes, some might minister for some time to certain pockets. But this is not a separate mission. For we all have one common mission. The church is just the place where all our missional activities converge, and the people of God gather together, irrespective of ethnicity. Now, if our missional strategy is first and foremost driven by Christ's command to reach people of all nations as we go about our daily business, then naturally this non-discriminatory evangelism strategy will be reflected in those that attend our local churches.

Hang on – can't we all just minister among certain cultural groups and allow Christ to unite us all together at the end of the age? Can it not be like a patch work quilt?

Surely not! For then we divide the body of Christ up based on nationalities. Is not the Scripture clear that we are neither Jew nor Gentile? Therefore, our identity is not based on nationalities. It is not that our cultural affiliations are not important; it is just that we all belong to a heavenly nationality that supersedes our own cultural identity. That is why we preach that 'our citizenship is in heaven. And we eagerly await a Saviour from there, the Lord Jesus Christ ...' (Phil 3:20).

Finally, dear brothers and sisters, here is a trustworthy saying: 'Because you are sons, God has sent forth the Spirit of His Son into our hearts, crying, "Abba! Father!"' (Gal 4:6). Consequently, if we are all adopted to be called his sons and daughters, and therefore heirs to the promises of our forefathers, then we are all welcome into the asylum of the Lord Jesus. And, if we are all welcome into his presence, then it is not by our skin colour, language or geography that we recognise one another, but by the same Spirit that cries Abba Father in all followers.

Therefore, let all those with the same Spirit meet together in fellowship.

TEN BIBLICAL REASONS WHY YOUR CHURCH MUST BE MULTIETHNIC

1. It remains the Father's vision for an asylum of all nations (Isa 56:7)

2. It is obedient to Christ's commission to reach all people from all nations (Matt 28:19; Acts 1:8)

3. Antioch is presented as the model church in the NT, made up of Jewish and Gentile nations (Acts 11:19–30)

4. The future asylum will be a multiethnic multitude from all nations (Rev 7:9; Isa 66:18–21)

5. Jesus is Lord of all the nations (Dan 7:13–14; Phil 2:5–11)

6. In Christ, the dividing walls have been broken down (Eph 2:14)

7. Jesus has died for people from every nation (Isa 11:10; Rev 5:9)

8. The apostles recognised the importance of the gospel going to the nations (Acts 10:34–35)

9. Through our forefather Abraham, God has blessed all nations (Gen 12: 3, 18:18, 28:14; Acts 3:25; Gal 3:8)

10. In Christ, we have a truly 'United Nation' asylum (Gal 3:28)

QUESTIONS FOR DISCUSSION

1. What can we learn from the asylum seekers in the Bible about how we should welcome strangers who come to our community, irrespective of ethnic background?

2. What lessons can we learn from the Old Testament about the treatment and segregation of Gentiles by the Jews of Jesus' day, as opposed to the inclusive nature of God's community?

3. What practical steps do you need to take to follow God's vision for your local church to become a 'house of prayer for all nations'?

4. What are the multiethnic principles we can learn from the church in Antioch as described in the book of Acts? How can these principles be applied in your local church today?

5. Does your local church reflect the vision of the church presented in Revelation 7:9?

6. How did the leaders of the early church resolve the tension between being a monoethnic community and a multiethnic community when faced with challenges like the Jerusalem Council (Acts 15)?

PART 2:
VISIONING THE ASYLUM

CHAPTER 6
THE AUSTRALIAN ASYLUM

> No one is born hating another person because of the colour of his skin, or his background, or his religion. People must learn to hate, and if they can learn to hate, they can be taught to love, for love comes more naturally to the human heart than its opposite. – Nelson Mandela[77]

Sunday 11 December 2005 will be remembered as one of the darkest days in Australia's history. A week after two Australian off-duty lifeguards were assaulted by a group of young men of Middle Eastern appearance, tensions erupted in Cronulla, a beachside suburb in Sydney's Sutherland Shire. Following days of heavy speculation, media coverage and a series of rallying text messages, a crowd gathered on that fateful Sunday morning to protest at Cronulla beach. Approximately 5,000 protesters, many fuelled by alcohol and carrying the Australian flag, took part in a series of sectarian clashes that became known as the Cronulla riots.[78]

These riots were the product of a ticking time bomb. For many years, New South Wales Police had recorded similar race-related attacks and bashings. There had been a history of conflicts and turf wars between locals and those visiting Cronulla from Sydney's western suburbs, 'Westies', dating even as far back as the 1960s.[79] In the aftermath of Cronulla, what is clear is that tensions between the two ethnic groups had been escalating from some time. As an example, just before the Sydney Olympics in 2000, coordinated racial rapes were carried out by a group of Lebanese Australian youth, perpetrated against Australian girls. These heinous crimes have been acknowledged by the majority of commentators as being ethnically motivated. The weight given to the racial aspects of the Sydney gang rapes by media outlets and politicians certainly fuelled the backlash and repercussions that subsequently led to Cronulla.[80] What can be said without a doubt is that since the events of 9/11, there have been heightened tensions between the Western world and those from Middle Eastern communities.[81] The Cronulla riots and the subsequent retaliations were a horrific example of these tensions between Anglo-Saxon (white, English speaking) Australians and those of Middle Eastern origin.

Unfortunately, when there's racial tension between two people groups, innocent bystanders fall in the crossfire. Furthermore, stereotypes start to form, and anyone who fits such categories becomes a target. For instance, the first attack during the Cronulla riots, occurring at 1.00 pm, was an assault of a man described as being of 'Middle Eastern appearance', who just happened to be on the beach that day. Several similar attacks took place against people of 'Middle Eastern appearance' right throughout the day. At 1.45 pm, two boys from Bangladesh were surrounded by the crowd and pelted by beer bottles while abusive slogans against 'Lebs' (Lebanese) were chanted. Subsequently, during the retaliation, car convoys full of Middle Eastern men travelled to the beaches and neighbouring suburbs to enact revenge. Reportedly carrying bats, guns, knives and machetes, they carried out a spate of attacks, assaulting several people and damaging property. A 26-year-old mechanic was left in a serious condition after being stabbed and kicked in the head. Another man was hit with a piece of concrete. Some of the vilest language and abuse was plastered across signs and t-shirts and echoed by the chanting crowd.

Police noted that in the week leading up to the riots there were some 270,000 rallying SMS text messages circulated among people from both sides, inciting racially motivated hostility. These messages contained such revulsion for another race that we have to ask ourselves, is this any different from the anti-Semitic propaganda of Nazi Germany? It is not befitting the nature of this book to dedicate any space to quoting such samples of the text messages, but the interested reader can do a simple Google search of the Cronulla riots and read them for themselves.

The Cronulla riots received widespread media coverage, locally and internationally. Traditionally, Australia had not been known for such violence. Since European colonisation first begun in 1788, Australia has not had a civil war or revolution. For the most part, Australia's involvement in international wars has seen the fighting restricted to foreign soil. Further, Australia has not experienced terrorism on the scale of its allied nations.[82] Nor have we experienced a breakdown in civil society or government. By and large, the fruits of democracy have flourished from coastline to coastline. Therefore, in the annals of Australian history, some commentators have suggested that the riots were just an exception in an otherwise peaceful land.

Yet this idea must be qualified. Despite the peace and prosperity Australians have enjoyed for the most part, this has not always been extended to the Indigenous members of the population. The Indigenous Australian population has experienced heavy decline due to the persecution inflicted during British colonisation and subsequent public policies. This persecution included the forcible removal of children from Aboriginal and Torres Strait Islander families, who were then placed in church-run missions or with other state government agencies. Although estimates vary, in some regions as many as one in three children were removed from their communities between the early 1900s until the mid-1960s, leading to a cohort of children known as the Stolen Generations. Oppression of a more violent nature included the massacre of waves of Indigenous Australians during frontier conflicts with European settlers.

Although Indigenous casualties were nationwide, some of the most infamous devastation took part during the 1820s and 30s in Tasmania. During a series of guerrilla-style struggles between colonists and the original inhabitants, known as the Black War, Tasmania experienced the almost complete annihilation of the island's Indigenous population. Only now, as more and more of this violence and racism is being uncovered, is its true extent being realised. In 2008, Australian Prime Minister Kevin Rudd issued a national apology to the Stolen Generations as part of a decades-long inquiry into the oppression of Indigenous families under the Commonwealth.

To this day, the consequences of these policies ripple through Australian society, with many Indigenous Australian communities still crippled with socio-economic challenges. This is truly a sad and shameful part of our nation's history. Only now is our nation starting to acknowledge it honestly and deal with the challenging questions surrounding redressing and bridging the gaps.[83]

No matter where you are from, each of you, and each society, will have a similar story of racial tension. Incidents like the Cronulla riots are proof that the church must rise up. They are proof that having a multiethnic framework for your church is not only a biblical mandate but also a cultural mandate. During the 1980s, John Stott published a book discussing the major issues affecting Christians today.[84] He dedicated a full chapter to discussing the 'multiracial dream'. In this chapter, he identified some of the worst cases of racism throughout the world. He concluded by stating that because of God's character, and because of what Christ has done, it is the church's obligation to create the model of harmony in society and pursue the multiracial dream.[85] Stott wrote,

> Only a true theology, the biblical revelation of God, can deliver us from racial pride and prejudice. Because he is God of Creation, we affirm the unity of the human race. Because he is the God of History, we affirm the diversity of ethnic cultures. Because he is the God of Revelation, we affirm the finality of Jesus Christ. And because he is the God of Redemption, we affirm the glory of the Christian church ... Because of the glory of the church, we must seek to rid ourselves of any lingering racism and strive to make it a model of harmony between the races, in which the multiracial dream comes true.[86]

Just as the words of Scripture should flow through the veins of our churches, a desire to create a model of the heavenly asylum should flow also. This is the way God intended the church to be. This is the church our society needs. In the midst of ethnic segregation, the church should be able to stand as a beacon of light, calling the world to a higher standard.

> You are the light of the world. A town built on a hill cannot be hidden. Neither do people light a lamp and put it under a bowl. Instead they put it on its stand, and it gives light to everyone in the house.

> In the same way, let your light shine before others, that they may see your good deeds and glorify your Father in heaven (Matt 5:14–16).

In the Great Commission, Jesus commanded his followers to go out and make disciples. In Australia, God has brought the nations to our shorelines. One of the reoccurring themes of the book of Daniel is the God who is sovereign over all nations and who orders the events of history to achieve his purposes. Australia is living proof of just how God has worked through global events to create a multiethnic society. What a privilege we have in our cultural context to minister among the nations. Just like no one can draw a picture of what the average Christian looks like, no one can paint a picture of the average Australian. From our appearances to our food preferences, we are diversity personified.

The evidence is in the statistics. The true nature of Australia's diversity can be seen in the 2011 census data, which reveal that more than one in four Australians were born overseas.[87] Even more incredibly, 43.1 per cent of people have at least one parent who was born overseas.[88] Moreover, in Sydney, Melbourne and Perth, more people come from families where both parents were born overseas than families where both parents were born in Australia.[89]

The breakdown looked like this in 2011: First generation Australians, those born overseas, totalled 5.3 million (27 per cent of the population). Second generation, those born in Australia with at least one overseas-born parent, numbered 4.1

million, representing 20 per cent of the population. Finally, third generation Australians, who are Australian born, with both parents Australian-born and at least one grandparent having been born overseas, 10.6 million, making up 53 per cent of the population. Consequently, sometimes people can be ignorant when making statements about immigration and ethnic diversity (like the signs held up during the Cronulla riots that claimed, 'We grew here, you flew here'), because they are unaware of Australia's true diversity. Australians come from over 300 ancestries![90]

We can't ignore the fact that Australia has always been a country built by immigration. Beginning with the original inhabitants of the land, those of Aboriginal or Torres Strait Islander ancestry were believed to have migrated from parts of South-East Asia and New Guinea around 50,000–60,000 years ago.[91] In 1788, Australia was settled as a Commonwealth colony with settlers and convicts emigrating from Great Britain. The discovery of gold, and subsequent gold rushes, sparked a period of rapid population growth in the mid-1800s. Immigration rates skyrocketed from an average of 12,000 arrivals yearly during the 1840s to over 50,000 in the 1850s. The period known as the gold rush era caused paramount change to Australia's economic, political and demographic makeup, with the population more than tripling from 430,000 in 1851 to over 1.7 million in 1871. Although the vast majority of migrants still came from the British Isles (about 500,000), some 60,000 people emigrated from areas of Continental Europe, 10,000 from the United States and about

5,000 from the South Pacific. Most noteworthy however, were the 40,000-plus industrious Chinese immigrants who came in pursuit of social advancement, many of whom faced racial discrimination and government restrictions.[92]

It was during this period that the seeds of multiculturalism started to sprout. It was during this period that God started preparing an infant nation for its journey towards becoming a country for people of all nations.

Unfortunately, our Commonwealth roots initiated arguably the darkest government policy in Australia's young history. The White Australia policy was a series of strategies and laws enacted by the newly federated government to discriminate against non-British migrants. These laws particularly targeted those from Asian and non-white backgrounds. A key feature was the *Immigration Restriction Act 1901*, which was designed to keep anyone from non-white backgrounds from immigrating. This included a dictation test administered by an immigration officer who could make a migrant sit the test in any European language, even if they didn't speak it. Accordingly, a white, Anglo-Australian society would dominate the first 40 years of the twentieth century, seeing off World War I and the Great Depression. Even as World War II began, anti-Japanese sentiment would see the Australian Prime Minster John Curtin rearticulate a desire for a white British Australia. However, the God of the nations would still have something to say. Much like God used the foreign policy of Cyrus, King of Persia, during Israel's exilic period, to accomplish his purposes, God was able to use Australia's changing immigration policy to provide a great opportunity for Australian churches.

Post-World War II Australian society and its views towards immigration rapidly changed. Feeling vulnerable after near-invasion by the Japanese, Australia adopted a new slogan, *'Populate or Perish'*, and assisted huge waves of migrants to arrive from across Europe, many of whom were displaced. Furthermore, the Anglo-Celtic immigration policy was relaxed due to labour shortages. From a population of just seven million after World War II, by 1965 Australia had surpassed 11 million. The government began offering incentives for new European migrants to resettle in Australia, though those from the UK continued to receive the greatest incentives. Literally year after year, the government would sign new treaties with European countries to boost migration. In 1946, agreements were signed with Britain, France, Belgium, Denmark, USA, the Netherlands and Poland, among others, to attract ex-servicemen. In 1948, peace treaties with countries like Italy, Hungary and Romania opened the way for new migrants.[93] In the two decades after World War II, although over one-third of post-war immigration still came from the UK and Ireland, other countries like Italy, Germany, the Netherlands, New Zealand, Greece, Malta, Austria, USA, Yugoslavia, Spain and Egypt began featuring more prominently.[94] In each of the six decades following World War II, Australia bought in close to one million migrants.[95]

During the 1970s, after the White Australia policy was formally dismantled, the government began forming a policy of multiculturalism. Since then, Australia has opened its doors to immigrants from all around the world, changing the face of society forever. Immigration from South-East Asian countries like Vietnam, the Philippines and Malaysia took off, due in large part to global events like the Indo-Chinese wars. By the time of the Sydney Olympics, New Zealand, China, Hong Kong, Vietnam, South Africa, India, Lebanon, Turkey and Yugoslavia had emerged as some of Australia's top sources for migrants.

Since 1945, over 7.5 million people have settled in Australia from overseas, with net immigration in recent years hovering around 190,000 annually. As of 2015, over 28 per cent of the population was born overseas.[96]

To this day in most areas of Australia, the multiethnic dream has flourished, with incidents like Cronulla proving to be nothing but mere footnotes in God's plan for a diverse Southern land. Nevertheless, some strong voices have still opposed aspects of a diverse Australia. One prominent example in the 1990s was federal parliament member Pauline Hanson. Hanson's views were that ordinary Australians were not being allowed to determine who came into our country and that Asians couldn't assimilate because of their culture and religion. The following is an extract from Hanson's maiden speech:

> I and most Australians want our immigration policy radically reviewed and that of multiculturalism abolished. I believe we are in danger of being swamped by Asians. Between 1984 and 1995, 40 per cent of all migrants coming into this country

were of Asian origin. They have their own culture and religion, form ghettos and do not assimilate. Of course, I will be called racist but, if I can invite whom I want into my home, then I should have the right to have a say in who comes into my country. A truly multicultural country can never be strong or united. The world is full of failed and tragic examples, ranging from Ireland to Bosnia to Africa and, closer to home, Papua New Guinea. America and Great Britain are currently paying the price.[97]

Admittedly, questions over how migrants are assimilated effectively and what countries they are coming from are fair questions that all national governments need to ask (especially given the contemporary challenges some countries are facing with the spread of radical Islam). All governments should exercise wisdom on such matters of public policy. It is also unfair to label people who are asking these questions as racists and bigots, as seems to be happening more and more in this politically correct culture.

I am not here to weigh in on that debate, only to point out that diversity provides a great opportunity for multiethnic churches. Nonetheless, what all churches should take aim at is any xenophobic attitude that refuses to believe that multiethnicity is something the Christian church can achieve. One of the reasons why I prefer the term 'multiethnic' to 'multicultural' is because a lot of people still have reservations and fears about a multicultural society. The church doesn't have the luxury of being xenophobic. The church in no way has any right to determine who enters our buildings; that's for God to decide.

Just as some may say that a multicultural country can never be strong or united, some church leaders think that a multiethnic church can never be strong or united. But where we are met with cynicism and doubt and by those who tell us that we can't, we will remind them that the New Jerusalem, the messianic kingdom, will be the exception to the rule. And it will be an exception that will last for all eternity.

Countries always struggle with the question of how to effectively integrate diverse people groups. Unfortunately, in Australia, the best way to do it has been to isolate people into pockets. In Sydney, for example, Cabramatta has been synonymous with Vietnamese people. Italians have traditionally lived around Five Dock and Leichhardt. Parramatta has attracted many people from India, while Bankstown has a lot of Middle Eastern people. The Northern Beaches has retained a traditional Anglo-Celtic population.

Naturally, when a person migrates to a new country, they want as best as possible to maintain their cultural identity and live around people who have emigrated from a similar region. Initially it is understandable that immigrants maintain close ties with people of a similar ethnicity; sometimes, given the language barrier, it can be unavoidable. In response, churches spring up to accommodate those community groups, encouraging and creating separate ethnic congregations. However, our long-term goal should never be to create homogenous churches. Rather, our strategy should be to integrate diverse community groups into our local churches. Otherwise, we develop the same problem that many homogenous churches today struggle with.

In the long run, monoethnic churches become ineffective and experience decline. We are already seeing this pattern in many churches, where second-generation members do not fit the monoethnic identity created by the original community. The young people eventually form their own identity based on what they experience outside the church. Every day at school, our kids are interacting with classmates from diverse backgrounds, yet when they go to church they are forced to mix with people of the same nationality. They may remain in these homogenous churches while they are young to appease their parents, but as they get older, they struggle to fit in. When the church doesn't mirror the diversity of the community, the second generation finds it harder to invite friends and reach out to those in the community. As a consequence, younger people disconnect from the church of their upbringing, and that church dies out.

Walk into any office, factory or government organisation in Australia and you'll see diversity. There is something wrong if our churches can't, or won't, reflect that same diversity. I mean, how bewildering is it that the world can model diversity better than the church? Even if homogenous worship helps first-generation immigrants to feel better connected with people from the same country, it doesn't help as they go in search of employment and connection to the wider society. Having a Mandarin or Cantonese service doesn't help your teenager, who would rather go to a church reflecting the same diversity seen in their school. Some monoethnic churches try rectifying this exodus by starting an English-speaking service to accommodate, but this doesn't correct the root problem monoethnic churches face when they fail to reflect the community.

The issue can be best concluded with this statement from John Stott. Referring to a conference sponsored by the Lausanne Movement in Pasadena, California, in 1977:

> There has been debate in recent years whether a local church could or should ever be culturally homogenous. A consultation on this issue concluded that no church should ever acquiesce in such a condition: 'All of us are agreed that in many situations a homogenous unit church can be a legitimate and authentic church. Yet we are also agreed that it can never be complete in itself. Indeed, if it remains in isolation, it cannot reflect the universality and diversity of the Body of Christ. Nor can it grow to maturity. Therefore, every homogenous unit church must take active steps to broaden its fellowship in order to demonstrate visibly the unity and the variety of Christ's Church'.[98]

Australia is one of the most multicultural countries in the world. Sydney is right up there as one of the most multicultural cities in the world. Therefore, there is no excuse for any church not to reflect that diversity.

There are some traditionalists who are trying to hold to the notion that Australia is still a Christian country. In actuality, such a statement is redundant, because there is no such thing as a Christian country to begin with. Although Australia, like parts of Europe and America, was traditionally heavily influenced by Judeo-Christian values, today it is very much a secular nation. In fact, Australia is becoming more and more secular, with rejection of the typical Christian values that use to form the ethos of society. We are not yet at the same point as Great Britain, but we a far removed from the patriotic Christianity which is still evident in the States. The main point of this chapter is to recognise that, in years to come, only churches that build on a foundation of God's word and vision for diversity will thrive in this increasingly diverse and secular society. In the previous section, we explored the biblical mandate for multiethnic churches. Now you've read about the sociological mandate for multiethnic churches.

The very words of our national anthem (which, by the way, was written by a Scottish immigrant) celebrate that, 'for those who've come across the seas, we've boundless plains to share'. Let the church be at the forefront of living out those words. Let those 'boundless plains' that we proclaim be the boundless plains of eternity and the boundless plains of the kingdom of God. If the church is truly going to be great, if the church is going to effectively live out our biblical and sociological mandate, then it is essential for us to model the diversity of Australia's multiethnic communities – on earth as it will be in heaven.

CHAPTER 7
PARKSIDE CHURCH

> I now realise how true it is that God does not show favouritism but accepts from every nation the one who fears him and does what is right. (Acts 10:34–35)

IN THE BEGINNING ...

Having looked at the biblical mandate for multiethnic worship, we turn now to look at how these ideals can start to be fleshed out in practice. This chapter contains the story of our multiethnic church, Parkside, as something of a test case for the multiethnic model.

In 2018, Savi and I celebrated 30 years of being together in ministry at Parkside. As any ministry family can surely attest, to spend three decades at one church is truly God ordained. Before coming to Parkside, we had been ministering at churches in the Sydney suburbs of Yagoona and Maroubra. There was a great temptation for me to stay pastoring in a beach suburb like Maroubra. But God just didn't want us there. He had other plans. We had a deep conviction to go where the need was greatest, so in 1988 we moved to Parkside Church.

The church is located in Edensor Park, New South Wales, a suburb in the Greater Western region of Sydney. The area is primarily a residential community, consisting mainly of middle-class families. What makes the area remarkable is that the City of Fairfield (the local government area) is one of the most ethnically diverse communities in the world. Fairfield itself is home to residents from all over the globe, with over half the population born outside of Australia. Our church is located on a busy suburban street; next door to us is a Laotian Buddhist temple. Also, visible from our church is a Turkish Mosque. An Assyrian club is a few hundred metres from the church. Behind us is a skate park. A couple of streets away are some public housing homes. Now, what I write next is no exaggeration. If you were to drive around the area for ten to fifteen minutes, you would be able to see three more Buddhist temples, an Islamic college, an Assyrian church, a Lebanese church, an Italian club, a Hungarian club, a Croatian club, a string of Asian restaurants ... I could go on.

To its credit, the local council identified several decades ago that the area was rapidly growing in diversity, and they have since then embraced the motto, *'Celebrating Diversity'*. Put simply, it doesn't get much more diverse than the area Parkside is in. The nations are truly at our doorstep. If the local council can celebrate and embrace diversity, how much more important it is for the local church to reflect this in the diversity of the congregation.

The original ministry at Parkside commenced in 1982 as an initiative of the Baptist Union of NSW to consolidate and grow the existing Christian ministries known as the Australian Migrant Mission and the Bossley Park Sunday School. The original fellowship was formally constituted as Parkside Baptist Church in June 1985, with a foundation membership of just 29 people. When we first arrived, the church had been operating for several years, but there remained only a handful of members. The original church building was basically a small shack, but this had been destroyed a year prior to our arrival by arsonists, so the members were using a temporary demountable building.

Although the area was fast becoming the ethnically diverse community we see today, the church remained primarily a traditional monoethnic Anglo community. We arrived with our young family to pastor a small congregation that didn't yet have a vision to reach the diverse community. From the very beginning, our desire and the vision that God put in our hearts was to see this congregation become a multiethnic asylum, effectively reaching the nations in the community.

The process began with educating the congregation about God's vision for a church made up of many nationalities.

Accordingly, I began to teach our people about multiethnicity and about God's plan to reach our diverse community through prayer meetings and Bible studies. The reason I believed the church didn't reflect the community was because the members didn't fully understand the nature and purpose of God's church. Therefore, I thought it was important to first establish the biblical mandate for a multiethnic church.

Before arriving at Parkside, God was already laying the foundations for the vision to take off. The dismantling of the White Australia Policy and the adoption of a new multicultural policy for immigration in Australia meant that the attitude of Australians was beginning to change. Also, global events like the Vietnam War meant that Australia started attracting new waves of immigration from South-East Asian and Middle Eastern countries.

One of the first things we did was to put together a ten-year vision for the church. It was a seemingly preposterous vision to become a church of over 1,000 people from at least 100 different nationalities. This was a big thing for the church, prior to which no official vision was evident. Within a few months, the church had used some of it savings to commence work on a new brick building to replace the demountable; this project was completed in 1990. We also conducted some research which idenitifed a major need in the community for a child care centre, and in 1989 we began running a preschool. This was a lot of hard work, but it allowed us to connect local families with the church community.

Throughout the 1990s the church experienced tremendous growth, and the existing facilities soon became inadequate to cater for this growth. In 2000, we adopted the motto of *'Building People for Eternity'*, with the plan to extend the existing facilities to accommodate for future growth. Work commenced on these new facilities in April 2003 and was completed in November of that year. The current facilities included an 800-seat auditorium, a function hall, children's ministry areas, living quarters, an administration area and upstairs offices, a café and a bookshop. The new facilities were officially opened in November 2003 by the then Attorney General of Australia, Philip Ruddock.

While this short overview may sound straightforward enough, these early years were filled with many difficult times. Yet God brought the right people at the right time and powerfully provided the funds needed. I want to emphasise, right from the beginning, that we knew God was with us and his faithfulness has never changed. It is my experience that whenever God takes you on a journey, he opens doors, and nothing can stand in your way. It doesn't mean the journey will be smooth sailing, but you will arrive at your destination. God is faithful in the little and the big things.

One of my first tasks upon arrival at Parkside was to negotiate with the relevant government agency for a land grant. We had a great space, though the building wasn't much. We just needed to secure the premises; with the development of so many new homes, schools and other elements of infrastructure, we were worried about losing it. At one time, we needed to put forward a bond of $7,500. We had one month and didn't know what to do. The small congregation just didn't have the funds needed. I even thought of finding extra work outside the church to raise the funds.

But I learnt that money is the least of God's problems! I remember arriving at our church one morning. It was pouring rain, mud everywhere. In the mail was a cheque for $10,000 from the estate of an anonymous lady. It reminded me that God is faithful in providing for our needs. In the words of James Hudson Taylor: 'God's work, done in God's way, will never lack God's supply'.

IN THIS WILDERNESS ...

During ministry development and formation, all young students are told to prepare for opposition in ministry. And all pastoral families can detail the struggles that they've faced in ministry. Subsequently, people often ask me about the types of resistance we've faced during our time at Parkside. Throughout any given day, pastors can literally find themselves on a rollercoaster of emotions. At the start of the day you could be celebrating with a family the birth of a child; by the end of the day you might be pastorally caring for a family experiencing grief after the loss of a loved one. One moment you could be rejoicing as someone is led to Christ; a few hours later you could be counselling someone whose partner has left them. It is just the nature of the job.

Nevertheless, building and sustaining a multiethnic church for 30 years has inevitably come with its own distinct difficulties. All churches are susceptible to clashes and divisions between different personalities. Most pastors will be familiar with church members who seem impossible to please. No matter how much you try to accommodate them, they complain about everything. If there's something they don't like about your church or your ministries aren't creative enough, they pack up and move on. Unfortunately, people like that approach church with a consumer-driven mentality. They think only about what church can do for them, rather than what they can do for the church. These issues are heightened when ministering among a diverse group of people. Our church has seen its fair share of people who didn't like what was going on and left. They were there one Sunday and gone the next.

We experienced resistance right from the start with some people opposed to the new direction in which Parkside was moving. I remember one occasion when a family came to me and informed me that they were leaving the church because the church had become 'too colourful' for their liking and they wanted to 'find another church with people just like them'. This may seem like a negative comment, but on the inside, I was delighted, because it meant that if the church was becoming noticeable for its colour then we were clearly moving in the right direction and in step with God's vision. On another occasion, a member who had been attending our church for several years notified me that he would be leaving the church and taking his family to a more rural community to avoid his children growing up in a multiethnic community.

In honesty, the greatest struggle has been battling against key people in the church who wanted Savi and me to pack up and leave because they didn't want a multiethnic church. There have been occasions where different leaders have outrightly rejected the vision and wanted me removed. In their disgruntled state, these leaders have sought to derail the vision and caused divisions in the church.

Then there are the challenges that members of our church experience daily and have to work through together by virtue of the multiethnicity of the church. For some people, the initial hurdle is a scriptural one. In their minds, reaching out to people from other ethnicities is a missionary task; they are happy for the church to fund or send missionaries overseas or even locally, but they don't see the need for the church to be multiethnic. They don't see anything wrong with having a church community made up of people from the same ethnic background. For many of these individuals they just need to be shown the biblical mandate for why a multiethnic community is part of God's salvation plan. Provided that is done with gentleness and respect, they will overcome their own personal struggles over time.

For others, the inner preference they have towards their own culture is the issue to they need to overcome. This may have to do with their upbringing and attitude towards certain ethnicities. For example, I have experienced some Anglo Australians who are indifferent towards Indigenous Australians. People with deeply ingrained biases towards certain ethnic groups find it hard to be part of any church that is open to all ethnicities. In my experience, this mentality is harder to eradicate in some ethnicities than others, and it might take some time to see this attitude changed.

The other major challenge individuals face, is even if they have a willingness to try and are proactive about getting to know people from different ethnic backgrounds, is navigating different cultural expectations. Expectation plays out in all sorts of areas of the life of the church. Many members of our church have their own stories about the first time they shared a meal with someone from a different background and had to navigate around the cultural barriers like different foods and eating customs. Things like marriage, raising children and respect for elders can become an issue between church members as different cultural perspectives emerge. Even matters surrounding conflict resolution can be tricky to deal with. Some cultures prefer to seek out a third party for mediation, while others don't address conflict openly at all. For many cultures, seeking counselling is a shameful thing, and this requires extra pastoral sensitivity.

These are just a small taste of some of the differing expectations within a multiethnic church. Much of what I have described here is not unique to a multiethnic setting; these are common struggles that many pastors will be familiar with in their own churches. But these challenges are certainly heightened in a multiethnic church setting, and navigating them as a community requires lots of patience, prayer and tolerance.

HE HAS WATCHED OVER YOUR JOURNEY ...

Today, Parkside is made up of over 600 members from over 60 different nationalities. When you walk into our auditorium you will see over 60 flags hanging along the walls. That is the heart of our church. Those flags represent the people of God's kingdom. Sitting atop our church building is a cross. It lights up blue at night time, shining out over the park behind us. Poetically, the cross from above and the flags inside together symbolise that this is God's house and inside are people from every tongue, nation and tribe.

Our main event every year, taking place in Spring, is our International Night. On International Night, we celebrate our diversity with multicultural food stalls, and we have a parade of nations with people waving their national flags and speaking and performing in their native language. We invite a guest speaker to come and share. It is a way for us to rehearse for the real International Night, which will take place daily in heaven. And it is also a place for us to be well fed. In past years, we've had World Vision CEO Tim Costello preach, and we've invited other dynamic Australian personalities, including television journalist Ray Martin and photographer Ken Duncan. But we don't just eat once a year. Every week our church runs a café on Sundays called Harmony Café. Each week on a rotating roster we have a different cultural group run the café.

Like most churches, we offer a variety of ministries and programs. Our youth group, Parkside Youth, runs on Friday nights. We have Sunday school programs and Synergy for young adults. Prime Timers is the name for our senior and retiree groups, for those over 50. Harvest is our ministry reaching families and those in middle age. SPICE is our ministry catering for the ever-growing singles demographic in our society. We run men's and ladies' groups monthly, and there are a variety of cell and home group Bible studies operating weekly.

A few years ago, we set up a charity organisation Just Care. Just Care is our local mission ministry, which reaches the local community through running events like barbeques, carols in the park and activities during the holiday period. Over the last few years through Just Care, we've run several skate competitions for local teenagers as a way of reaching them in the skate park. We also identified that learning to speak English is one of the greatest needs for the many immigrants moving into the area, so we've run English conversation classes for them. We are very intentional about making sure that all our ministries adequately model the diversity of the church. Therefore, all our ministries contain a deliberate multiethnic feel and diversity in representation, from the church pastors, leaders and deacons to the worship team and multimedia.

We presently operate with two services on Sundays. They are always in English and open to all ages. In recent times we have started to incorporate different languages into parts of our worship and singing: our worship team will sing a couple of verses or a chorus from a well-known worship song in another language like Hindi, Spanish, Hebrew or Arabic. We will include the lyrics of the language on the screen. Because the song is always a well-known one in Christian circles, most people will easily identify what the words mean. The worship band will then revert back to English.

We are very particular about maintaining the multiethnic ethos of the church. In the past we have been approached by groups asking us to form monoethnic services and separate congregations. We don't allow this, because it goes against the overall vision and strategy of the church. We also don't encourage or promote monoethnic home groups. If individuals wish to host a weekly home group, then we encourage them to open it up to people from other ethnicities.

Currently our mission is to be 'a Christian Community Committed to Making Christ Known to People of All Nations'. The vision is to be a vibrant community of more than 2,000 members from over 100 different nationalities, and we desire to see people from every culture in our community come to know the LORD and worship together as one big family of God's people. My prayer is for Parkside to continue to be an asylum for those who seek to settle in this beautiful country and know God.

Ministering in a diverse context like Parkside comes with great joys. As I constantly remind the congregation, this will be what we see in heaven. There will be no greater spectacle for the eternal ages than when that vision of Revelation 7:9 is fulfilled and every tongue, nation and tribe is worshipping before the throne of God. And the joy of living out that vision, even in our small way, is more satisfying than any of the opposition that sometimes comes with ministering among the nations.

Admittedly, there have been times when we've been so overworked that I've missed seeing that diversity flourish. Sometimes we focus on the problems and this prevents us from seeing what God is doing. Yet when someone from outside comes into the church and comments on the diversity at Parkside, I've noticed God's work afresh. Those moments make up for all the difficult times. It is then that I'm reminded of the significance of what we're doing and glad that God called us to be a part of his story. The greatest moments come when people are led to the LORD. It was a great joy when, on one occasion, I was able to baptise 26 people from 20 different ethnic backgrounds.

Throughout the years, we have been supported by several people who have strongly embraced the vision of the church. They have encouraged us, prayed for us and worked tirelessly at times to grow the church. Without God placing them in our path, Parkside wouldn't be what it is today, and Savi and I would not have enjoyed the longevity that we have experienced at Parkside.

Finally, as you can imagine with such diversity under one roof, there have inevitably been some humorous occasions. I will share one memorable story. On this occasion, an African lady came to the church and asked for prayer because she was trying to get pregnant. After praying for her, we took communion and she went on her way. A few weeks later she came by, overjoyed and proclaiming that she was pregnant. She began telling everyone before the service that she was pregnant because the pastor had given her some magical bread and wine. As we started the service, she was dancing up and down the isles praising God. This was a new experience for our church congregation; we had not seen this emotive style of rejoicing, which is very prominent in African worship. She started attending our church, and I dedicated her baby. I still don't know whether she thought I was some kind of witch doctor or whether she thought communion was a concoction capable of making someone pregnant!

I feel strongly that the story of our church must be told. A friend of mine, Tim Costello, told me that despite being to so many churches, he has never seen anything as remarkable as Parkside. When it comes to putting multiethnic ministry into practice, Parkside is one among several asylums around the world leading the way, and we've realised that it is our obligation to share the knowledge and experience that we've gained with other churches who are in similar positions, trying to grow a multiethnic church.

QUESTIONS FOR DISCUSSION

1. What should be the Christian response be toward government immigration policies that clearly discriminate against people on the basis of ethnicity (Acts 10:34–36)?

2. What lessons can we learn from existing multiethnic churches (like Parkside) about an integrated community of God's people, all worshipping, working and walking together as one body of Christ?

3. What dangers emerge when a local church doesn't reflect the demographics of the local community? What steps can the church take to address this disparity?

PART 3:
GATHERING THE ASYLUM

CHAPTER 8
BUILDING A MULTIETHNIC ASYLUM

Part 3 marks a shift in the focus of the book. For many years I've been mentoring other pastors about multiethnic ministry and I've spoken at other churches, conferences and colleges here in Sydney and around the world. Other churches and its leaders have sought out Parkside to learn about how to build and sustain multiethnic ministries. Therefore, the next three chapters are about putting some of the lessons learnt into practical application. Here we must navigate our way around three of the more practical questions that our asylum seekers will face in building, sustaining and leading a multiethnic church.

Imagine a multiethnic church to be like a three-legged stool. One leg is the biblical foundation, the second leg is relational community, and the final leg is diverse leadership. These are the three foundational truths of a multiethnic church.

[Diagram: A three-legged stool labeled "Multiethnic Church" on the seat, with legs labeled "Biblical Foundation," "Relational Community," and "Diverse Leadership."]

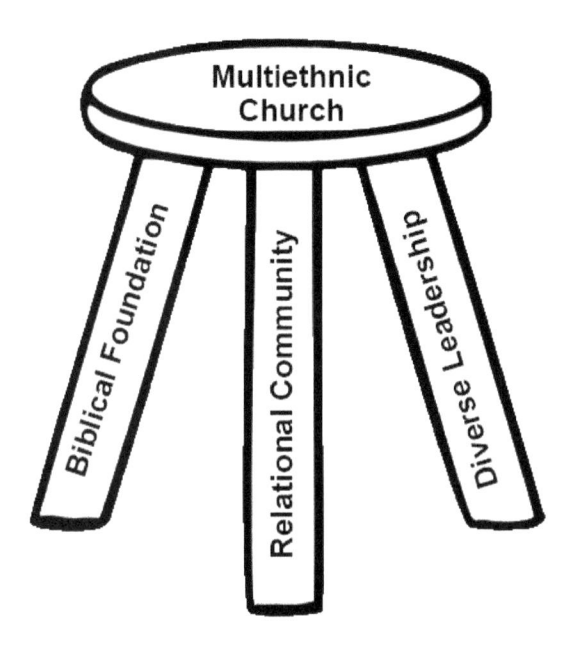

We've already looked at the first leg, the biblical foundations, in our discussion of the scriptural mandate for multiethnic churches in Part 2. In Part 3, we address the other two legs. Chapter 9 examines the creation of a relational community. Chapter 10 addresses the question of diverse leadership.

Before we can get there, however, we need to lay the foundation by exploring some of the key steps that churches should take in order to transform a monoethnic church into a multiethnic church. As you can imagine building a multiethnic church is not for the faint heartened. It is even harder to transform a homogeneous church into a multiethnic church. As I identified in chapter 7, we found ourselves in that very position upon our arrival at Parkside. Accordingly, I want to share with you the seven steps we applied when building a multiethnic church at Parkside. Each of these steps is easily adoptable and refinable depending on your specific context. Although there will inevitably be distinct challenges leaders will encounter in each phase.

Let me start with a qualification. These guidelines are principles a church planter should adopt from the very beginning. For those trying to transform a monoethnic church into a multiethnic one, these steps should be gradually implemented. Some can be put in place straight away, while others will take some time. It will be up to a particular church's pastors and leaders to identify when they believe the church congregation is ready for these changes to take place. If leaders are searching for a rough timeline, my experience at Parkside suggests that you should be well on your way to implementing these steps within the first twelve months. Keep revisiting these principles, and make it a priority to take the congregation along with you for the journey. The hope is that, over months and years, these principles will take root and your church will slowly grow from a monoethnic congregation into a multiethnic asylum.

SEVEN STEPS FOR BUILDING A MULTIETHNIC ASYLUM

1. HAVE CONVICTION

By now I hope that you've reflected on the main point I've established: God's asylum is multiethnic! God's communicated purpose for the church and the example of the early church should reinforce our desire to strive for multiethnic church models. Therefore, the first step requires you and your leadership team to have a personal conviction to reach people of all nations. If your heart is set upon reaching only people of your kind, then that's what you'll end up doing. But if you're truly reflecting on the Scriptures and submitting yourself to God's purposes, then he will bring conviction to your heart to reach people of all nations.

When my wife and I made the decision to come to Parkside, we both had a strong conviction in our hearts that this is where God wanted us. We didn't go there because our denomination asked us to go or simply because we both wanted a sea change. Moreover, we made a long-term commitment of ten years to the church community. We knew that we needed to make that sort of long-term commitment to see God's vision for the community fulfilled. At times, it was tough to honour that commitment. I had a young family, and the church could not afford to pay a full-time salary. We had no permanent building in which to conduct our services and were meeting in a demountable. We had limited financial resources and personnel. It quickly became apparent to me that to be an effective leader, I must have a personal conviction and be bound to God's mission, submitting my thoughts and plans to his will.

If your loyalty lies with contributing to God's kingdom, that will grow into a willingness to be sacrificial. Peter and the account of Cornelius the Roman centurion, who became an early Gentile convert to Christianity, is a good example of such personal conviction (Acts 10). Peter was challenged by a vision from God that changed his whole mindset about evangelising people beyond his own ethnicity. This change of conviction was demonstrated when he said, 'I now realise how true it is that God does not show favouritism but accepts people from every nation who fear him and do what is right' (Acts 10:34–35). His prior attitude had been that it was against the law for him to mix with non-Jews (Acts 10:28).

Those who successfully lead organisations know that a business never goes beyond the strength and determination of its leaders. Without fail, any vision for change goes nowhere unless the leaders themselves believe in the idea. Unlike secular organisations, the leadership in the church must rely on God. During times of crisis, it is a deep conviction and commitment to God's calling that urges leaders to stay in ministry. Conviction is simply part of team conditioning. No sporting team can achieve victory unless they first have the conviction to win; likewise, conviction is an integral part of the Christian mission.[99]

Martin Luther King once brilliantly communicated a biblical understanding of conviction in a sermon entitled, 'But If Not'. Throughout this sermon he articulated that even in the face of imprisonment, his conviction told him that racism and segregation was wrong. He preached about the story of Shadrach, Meshach and Abednego (Daniel 3), in particular the conviction that they held for God in spite of the dangers they faced at the hands of king Nebuchadnezzar: 'But if not, be it known unto thee, O king, that we will not serve thy gods, nor worship the golden image which thou hast set up' (Dan 3:18 KJV).

Jesus demonstrated the greatest example of conviction at Gethsemane (Matt 26:36–46). Despite feeling abandoned (Matt 26:31–35) and grieved by the burden of sin and the cup of suffering placed on him, his conviction was fixated on the will of God the Father: 'Father, if you are willing, take this cup from me; yet not my will, but yours be done' (Luke 22:42).

Our convictions never will be as entirely submissive to the will of God as Jesus' was. That's a process God will always be working in us to achieve. But you can trust that he will light the passion within you to move your church in a multiethnic direction.

2. DEEPEN KNOWLEDGE OF YOUR COMMUNITY

All church planters' prioritise this step, and most likely your church already does so too.

In building a multiethnic church, it is vital to get to know the community. Yet we must be particularly careful not to be biased in this effort. It is possible to look at the community around us and see people of our own kind instead of embracing the whole community. In the past, some churches in the church growth movement have unhelpfully created stereotypes of people in their community with descriptions of the 'average Joe' and have sought to model church on attracting such a person. From this model, many seeker-sensitive churches have emerged. The problem with this mindset is that the Great Commission tells us exactly the parameters of the people we need to reach – *people of all nations*. Multiethnic churches don't appeal to niche markets; they are for mass markets! For this reason, a multiethnic church is harder to grow and nurture.

The church's evangelistic target should not be about just reaching only the 'average' person in the community. In fact, Jesus' model was to reach out to the more marginalised, not the typical person (Matt 9:10–17; Mark 2:15–22; Luke 5:29–39). Evangelistic approaches once endorsed by megachurches like Saddleback and Willow Creek require churches to gather information on the average person and create composite profiles like 'Saddleback Sam' and 'Saddleback Samantha', yet as popular as these approaches were, this is not the biblical model.[100] Can you imagine Jesus creating a character profile of 'Justin Jew' or 'Jane Jew' as his target group? Interestingly, the religious leaders in Jesus' day were against him eating with sinners because they didn't fit the typical 'righteous person' profile. Jesus was about reaching all people, because all people were sinners. The trouble with monoethnic churches is that they inadvertently do the same as the religious leaders by creating an exclusionary character profile based on ethnicity.

Some people might see broadening the evangelistic target as an impossible task, thinking it is unrealistic or naïve to try to reach all people. As Rick Warren wrote in the mid-1990s:

> Too many congregations are naive in their thinking about evangelism. If you ask the members, 'Who is your church trying to reach for Christ?' the response will likely be 'Everybody! We're trying to reach the entire world for Jesus'. Of course, this is the goal of the Great Commission, and it should be the prayer of every church, but in practice there is not a local church anywhere that can reach everybody ... For your church to be most effective in evangelism you must decide on a target. Discover what types of people live in your area, decide which of those groups your church is best equipped to reach, and then discover which styles of evangelism best match your target.[101]

There is some merit to Warren's view. Yes, individual churches are incapable of reaching everyone. Yes, when you have large concentrations of people all sharing the same socio-economic or ethnic demographics, the church ought to be mindful of this for evangelism purposes. But the weakness of this thinking is that it uses the language of commercialism and person-centeredness to describe the advancement of the gospel. Jesus is not a product that needs to be packaged based on an individual's personal preferences. Jesus isn't like a genre of music that some people like and others don't. It isn't about attracting certain people to a church, it is about attracting all people to Jesus.

In my experience, the seeker-sensitive church model and character profiling was never successful at Parkside because the community was too diverse. We couldn't create a 'Parkside Peter' married to a 'Parkside Pam' with three children. In our community, we were more likely to find names such as Haddad and Nguyen.

This call to avoid character profiling should not stop you from studying your community in order to identify the demographics of the people in your neighbourhood for practical purposes. In Acts 17:16–32, Paul certainly did his market research. We are told that upon entering Athens, he surveyed the area, carefully observing the city, finding it to be full of idols, at which point he became greatly distressed. His resulting action was to go out to the common places where the people were, in the synagogues and the marketplace and the Areopagus. Luke even sharply observes one of the favourite pastimes of the Athenian people and its foreigners: 'All the Athenians and the foreigners who lived there spent their time doing nothing but talking about and listening to the latest ideas' (Acts 17:21). Presumably Paul observed this habit (or knew about it already) and uses it for the advancement of the gospel. The Scriptures even show God doing his market research (metaphorically speaking!). During the conversation which took place when Abraham was appealing to the Lord to spare Sodom (Gen 18:16–33), God essentially told Abraham that he'd studied the people of Sodom demographically and had already identified that they were a wicked people whose sins were great. God told Abraham that he would continue researching the city to see if even ten righteous people were present, before taking the next appropriate action.

The research we conducted initially at Parkside highlighted two main facts. Firstly, cultural and ethnic transitions had resulted in people from over 160 nations migrating to the area. Our local area had become one of the largest multiethnic communities in Australia and around the world. As a result, the local council, Fairfield City, had changed its motto to *'Celebrating Diversity'*. In the last chapter, we mentioned just some of the buildings you would see if you drove around our community. These are all cultural centres that have sprung up because of the community's growing diversity over the past four decades.

Secondly, there were a growing number of young families moving into Edensor Park and the neighbouring suburbs. Subsequently, one of the vital needs for these young families was child care. Although the community was rapidly developing, child care was still in short supply. Accordingly, we completed the relevant government requirements and began operating a preschool as a means of catering for this essential need. This provided not only an opportunity to build the church's rapport with the locals but presented an enormous opportunity to bring new families into the church. The running of the preschool, although a tremendous amount of work, proved to be a major factor driving the rapid growth that we experienced in those early years. Through this initiative, God took us from a small congregation to a more vibrant multiethnic congregation. We accompanied this ministry with other initiatives to better connect the community, including starting a play time and youth group. We entered schools to teach Scripture and went door knocking with information packages for new home owners. The packages included the bus and train timetables, a calendar and some information about our church. These ministries helped the church better connect and serve the needs of the community.

I would encourage leaders seeking to grow a multiethnic church to exegete your local area and get to know prominent community leaders such as local mayors, the police, schools and council departments. Spend time walking around the shops to see what activities people are engaging in. Take your leaders around the community with you. Pay attention to local and national surveys like the Australian census; become acquainted with sites that provide relevant data like the Australian Bureau of Statistics and the National Church Life Survey.

The members of your church are often the best source of information but having a good relationship with local bodies is beneficial in the long run, because you can tap into vast amounts of resources. Getting to know the needs of the community and having close ties with external organisations has been the best way for the church to engage with the community. From these relationships we have been able to run things like Scripture classes, skate comps, ESL classes, Christmas carols and other public holiday events.

What if the surrounding community is monoethnic?
Many pastors over the years have asked me how the church can look different if the community looks the same. They've said things like, 'The demographics of my church represent those in the community', or, 'My church is monoethnic because the community is'. One gentleman asked me this question at a conference. I asked him if his local shopping centre had a Chinese restaurant. He said yes. How about an Indian one? He replied yes again. How about a Lebanese restaurant, or an Asian bakery, or ... I continued to list several other things. To every single one, he replied yes. So, I naturally asked him, who runs these places? Are you sure your community is monoracial? Or have you only identified one specific group of people in your community?

On another occasion, a fellow pastor and friend once lamented to me that his church was struggling to grow. I took him to the nearby shops for a coffee and asked him to look around and tell me what he saw. As people walked past, going about their business, I asked him if these were the same types of people he was seeing weekly at his church. He said no. Why was this the case? Because he was trying to run a monoethnic church in a multiethnic community.

There are a couple of lessons we can learn from these scenarios. The first one is easy: never presume the community is monoethnic. In both scenarios, the pastors had not done a proper study of the community. Unfortunately, in my experience, many churches fall into the trap of falsely believing that they represent the area, when truthfully, if you walk out on the street, they don't.

Secondly, if it *is* the case that your immediate community is quite homogenous, then explore other communities beyond your local neighbourhood. Chances are other suburbs still within driving distance represent a more diverse community. If we consider Sydney as an example, there are many suburbs that are monoethnic. Close to Parkside is the suburb of Cabramatta, which has a high concentration of Vietnamese people. Several churches in this area are monoethnic, with Vietnamese congregations. Yet Parkside is less than a five-minute drive away operating a multiethnic church.

Finally, if after conducting extensive research you still believe your church has done all it possibly can to reach a diverse range of people, but the local community just isn't multicultural enough, then you must ask yourself why that is. Are these suburbs 'gated communities'? Do they represent a deeper level of division between ethnicities? If so, it is imperative for the church not to model this same fracture. It must be the church's mission to be the source of light in that segregated community. Modelling the same fractured relationships between different ethnicities doesn't serve the community.

There are many suburbs in Sydney that have, I fear, become cultural ghettos, in which people from certain cultures have tried to maintain a closed community. We have already mentioned Sydney's Sutherland Shire in chapter 6. Many in this beachside suburb are prideful of the traditional Anglo nature of the community and look down on others from less affluent areas. They label people as 'Westies'. No matter where you are around the world, you will have observed similar cases of class warfare.

Jesus never told us to model the church on the demographics of Jerusalem. Instead, the church is to be the place where ethnic and socio-economic barriers are broken. Gated communities existed also in Jesus' day. The Jews didn't want to have anything to do with the Samaritans, so they avoided the region. Yet in John 4, Jesus made a point of going through Samaria, because he wanted to extend his mission strategy beyond the local Jewish communities. And the specific reference to being witnesses in Samaria (Acts 1:8) challenges the 'gated suburb' mentality, because Jesus knew that Samaria was a place where Jews typically didn't want to go. We in the church can focus all our attention on reaching the 'Jerusalems' we are in and sending missionaries to the ends of the earth, but we can all too quickly forget about Samaria. To effectively live out Jesus' commands, we must reach all three.

3. CREATE AN INCLUSIVE MISSION AND VISION

'Where there is no revelation, people cast off restraint' (Prov 29:18).

This proverb has been widely adopted in common usage, often phrased colloquially: 'Where there is no vision, the people perish'. Although such rendering is technically a mistranslation, the point stands. A church needs a vision and a mission. As noted already, a complete absence of vision was one of the primary issues hindering church growth at Parkside when Savi and I arrived. There was no mission statement or clear direction that the church was heading in. While many in the church loved the LORD, there was no formal statement by the members about where they wanted Parkside to go.

My first response was to make clear to the members that unless we established a vision that was in line with the word of God, our church community would not grow. Looking at the biblical mandate for mission, I put together a mission statement and presented it to the leadership: 'Our mission is to be a Christian community committed to sharing Christ with people of all nations'. This was not a new mission theology I had invented; this was a reaffirmation of the mission given by Jesus in Matthew 28, to make disciples of all nations.

Ideally everyone who serves at your church must be aware of the church's mission statement. The phraseology 'all nations' is the key, because it communicates the church's primary objective. The mission of Jesus is inclusive; it embraces people from every ethnic background. Becoming a multiethnic community begins with an intentional mission statement reaffirming the desire to reach people from all ethnic backgrounds.

Here the reader is encouraged to read Appendix 1 for a closer examination of the homogenous unit principle. Multiethnic churches must be built around a heterogenous mission model.

4. EDUCATE THE CONGREGATION

> These are the commands, decrees and laws the LORD your god directed me to teach you to observe in the land that you are crossing the jordan to possess ... these commandments that i give you today are to be on your hearts. Impress them on your children. Talk about them when you sit at home and when you walk along the road, when you lie down and when you get up. Tie them as symbols on your hands and bind them on your foreheads. Write them on the doorframes of your houses and on your gates (DEUT 6:1–9).

Some leaders may experience worry about how members will respond to the church becoming more multiethnic. As I've shared, in the past we have encountered some congregation members who did not applaud the decision to become multiethnic. Today, we are also aware that some cultures can find it harder to integrate than others.

The only way to bring your church on board is to open up the Scriptures and invite dialogue. This dialogue must be presented at the pulpit, in Bible study groups and at periodical events like church meetings and camps. In fact, to make moves towards a new vision without communication with the congregation is not in line with the spirit of a priesthood of all believers.

Moses' declaration in Deuteronomy 6 laid down the commitment to teach the people about what God has commanded.

Unfortunately, one of the key reasons why the people of God failed, time and time again, was that this imperative had been ignored. New generations of Israelites were born, and no one taught them the ways of the LORD (see Judg 2:10). Eventually in the nation's story, it got to the point where nobody knew God's word. Isaiah, using the illustration of a sealed scroll, comments that the people remain ignorant of God's words: 'The LORD says: "These people come near to me with their mouth and honour me with their lips, but their hearts are far from me"' (Isa 29:13).

Whenever you seek to invite transformation within the life of the church, it cannot merely be done behind the scenes, nor can it just be done at the pulpit. In our experience, the concept of a multiethnic church was new for many people in the congregation. The idea of different ethnic groups worshipping together in one place was a strange concept. There weren't any manuals and textbooks to consult to help the process. There were no other examples of multiethnic congregations to point to. Accordingly, I had to invest the early part of my ministry in teaching the congregation. I spent the first year of our ministry at Parkside presenting arguments from Scripture to the church about the multiethnic mandate, accompanying what was being said on Sunday with Bible study material, which I prepared and gave to home group leaders to ponder, discuss and pray about in their weekly home groups. Without such devotion to education, how can the congregation capture the vision?

It is vital to acknowledge that there are different barriers and resistances people experience during the education process.

Some members of the congregation more readily embrace the vision, while others take longer. Different barriers can only be addressed as they come, but in Appendix 2 we touch briefly on some of the barriers people have towards a multiethnic mission.

5. TAKE INTENTIONAL AND INCREMENTAL STEPS

This is the stage where your church has to start looking more multiethnic. Over time the church community must make progressive changes, some of which will have extremely large implications. This is where the multiethnic philosophy hits the road in a practical way. A multiethnic church does not just happen overnight; it takes intentional steps and incremental strides. By intentional, we mean premeditated, strategic and deliberate changes that indicate the multicultural direction in which your church is heading. By incremental, we mean making changes progressively, gradually and steadily, always bearing in mind the foundational work and training that must be done before proceeding.

Mark DeYmaz helpfully reminds us that, in ministry, dependency and intentionality are different sides to the same coin.[102] We are dependent on God, but with that dependency God expects us to partner with him and make intentional decisions with the wisdom he has given to us.

> ... although we did believe it was up to the Holy Spirit to make the dream come true, we did not believe this was an excuse to abandon further concern or

to abdicate personal responsibility in pursuit of a healthy multiethnic church. On the contrary; although prayer is foundational, partnership with Christ is fundamental to the effort and must lead us to make purposeful decisions along the way. I can assure you wishful thinking will not get the job done! There are, indeed, some things we can and must do to make the dream come true.[103]

Progressively, you will need to start making major changes. The overall objective is to start integrating different ethnic groups within your church and developing diverse leadership. Those within the church must intentionally start inviting people from different ethnic backgrounds from the local community to the church. You must then include people from these different backgrounds in the day-to-day running of the church. They must be actively encouraged and given opportunities to serve and lead ministries. They must be involved in the decision making, the visioning and direction of the church and incorporated into church meetings and planning sessions. To be truly multiethnic, it isn't enough just to have people from different backgrounds attending; those same individuals must also be the ones actively moving the church forward. In this phase, the church must start to remove former traces of monoethnic ministries. This requires bringing ethnically-based worship services or segregated activities together.

For churches that have different ethnic congregations worshipping separately and at different times, which was not our situation at Parkside, this requires long-term planning, and everyone must be on board. For a discussion of how to deal with the language barrier and integrating multiple services together over time, see Appendix 3.

At Parkside, the first intentional thing we did was to put up greeting signs in different languages. Eventually, when the new building was constructed, the signs were replaced by flags. We now have over 60 flags on display, representing the different nationalities that make up our church. Whenever a newcomer walks through the doors, the first thing we want them to see is that people of all nations are welcomed. Whenever a new person joins our community, we make it a point of hanging their nation's flag if it isn't already there. This may seem like a small step, but it sends a bold message to people.

The second intentional thing we did was to begin celebrating diversity as a community. Once a month, we set aside a Sunday to celebrate the different ethnic groups in our community and to build awareness. This was a great space for people to share their story and offer different foods and cultural presentations. Eventually, it became our yearly international night.

Another intentional step was to encourage people from different ethnic backgrounds to start interacting with one another. Opportunities were given to people to do this in various ministry settings. To be a multiethnic church, we had to become a welcoming and hospitable community. It was important we had a good welcoming team, and we implemented a 'five-minute rule'. The five-minute rule encourages all people to spend the first five minutes after the Sunday service talking to someone they haven't spoken to before.

In Act 2:5, it says, 'Now there were staying in Jerusalem God-fearing Jews from every nation under heaven'. By the end of the chapter, as the church radically starts to grow, Luke notes:

> They devoted themselves to the apostles' teaching and to fellowship, to the breaking of bread and to prayer. Everyone was filled with awe at the many wonders and signs performed by the apostles. All the believers were together and had everything in common. They sold property and possessions to give to anyone who had need. Every day they continued to meet together in the temple courts. They broke bread in their homes and ate together with glad and sincere hearts, praising God and enjoying the favour of all the people. And the Lord added to their number daily those who were being saved (Acts 2:42–47).

The more people from different ethnic backgrounds meet and interact, the stronger the unity becomes. At Parkside, Savi and I spent a lot of time opening our home and inviting people from different ethnic backgrounds to join us. Our home became a mini-model of a multiethnic church. We encouraged other people to do the same.

As I've already mentioned, we also ask different cultural groups to run our café each week. This gives people a chance to enjoy different cuisines and fellowship with one another over a meal. Furthermore, we promote inclusive weekly home groups where no single nationality dominates. We also encourage all ministry leaders to intentionally seek out and develop leaders from diverse backgrounds.

Part of being intentional means being aware when people are falling into an exclusive 'clique' mentality. For instance, if I ever observed, after the service, groups forming with people from the same ethnic background, I intentionally started introducing other people into the group to change the dynamic. Over the years, we've had many groups approach our church seeking to set up a separate monoethnic congregation. We have never allowed that to happen. Part of the reason for this is in a multiethnic church, we cannot have different monoethnic groups functioning separately. It would be counterproductive. We never want the church to be divided into different ethnic congregations. We want our church to be a house of prayer for all nations.

In this regard, we were fortunate to have a neutral name, Parkside, because the church was named after the surrounding suburbs that included the word 'park' (Edensor Park, St Johns Park, Bossley Park, Horsley Park). Eventually, the council built a park right next to the church and invited me to speak at the dedication. A neutral, generic name like Parkside is a great blessing because it is unrestrictive. It opens up opportunity for people from different ethnic backgrounds and even denominations to join without any reservations.

Often, a key hinderance in monoethnic communities becoming multiethnic is the very way the community labels itself. As the old expression goes, there's a lot in a name. If you have a monoethnic name like Western Chinese Church, Timbuktu Lebanese Church or Eastern Russian Orthodox Church, you are limiting the scope of who you are trying to reach from the start. Although we are a Baptist church, at Parkside the thing we want to project to the community is not an exclusive denomination but Christ. We want to be known in the community as a church inclusive of all nations.

6. INVITE DIVERSE LEADERSHIP

I will go deeper into the theory and practicalities of diverse leadership in chapter 10. Accordingly, I will not say any more about diverse leadership and multiethnic ministry at this point, other than to leave the reader with a taste.

Multiethnic ministry means multiethnic leadership. All ministries must have an intentional multiethnic flavour to them, from the pastoral team and deacons to those working in the café and the bookshop. The diversity you want from your congregation is the same diversity you must model in the leadership. The more diverse the leadership team is, the better equipped the church will be at leading the diverse community. Over the years, we've been very intentional in recruiting, training and equipping people from different backgrounds to be involved in our various ministries. Keep in mind that the early church in Acts 6 purposefully selected seven Hellenised leaders to help accommodate the growing needs of the believers, who were fast becoming a booming multiethnic community with heterogeneous needs. So, earnestly pray for and seek out diverse leadership.

7. ESTABLISH CROSS-CULTURAL RELATIONSHIPS

In the formative years at Parkside, we stressed to the congregation the importance of making the effort to get to know people from other cultures. It could not be just about my family opening our home to others; everybody needed to be doing this.

Another important component of this is pursuing cross-cultural competence. Building a vibrant multiethnic community requires a decent amount of knowledge of cultures different to our own. Every culture has its own unique language, customs, perspectives, traditions, values, expressions of church and expectations. Cross-cultural competency therefore relates to the ability and awareness of leaders to understand how those categories differ between cultural groups and engage effectively with other cultures. While no person can obtain expert knowledge about all cultures, cross-cultural ministry does require an appropriate aptitude and capacity to study other cultures. It is imprudent to foster assumptions that all cultures are similar and that what works well with some cultures will work well with any culture. As Mark DeYmaz and Harry Li note,

> To build a healthy multiethnic church, we must commit ourselves to the pursuit of cross-cultural competence, whether that means becoming proficient in the idiosyncrasies of language or learning the ins and outs of traditions different from our own. Once acquired, cross-cultural competence allows us to interact in a more informed and effective way with others of various ethnic of economic backgrounds. In many ways, cross-cultural competence is more caught than taught.[104]

DeYmaz and Li are correct in suggesting that learning about other cultures can often be more caught than taught. By this I mean, more often than not, that you learn on the go. Nonetheless, the very purpose of training and equipping leaders from a variety of ethnic backgrounds is to increase the whole community's understanding of other cultural groups. Blind spots are everywhere in ministry. By incorporating others who come from different backgrounds, our blind spots are reduced. And obviously, the best way to get to know another person's culture is to build a relationship.

Even in the days of the early church, conscious efforts were made to build bridges between different cultures. In the first century, it was considered culturally unacceptable for a Jew to eat and fellowship with non-Jews, let alone to enter the home of a Gentile (Acts 10:28). For this reason, Peter was hesitant when God was reshaping his perceptions towards the Gentiles

(Acts 10:14). However, amid these cultural barriers, the gospel still flourished.

The actions of Philip and the Ethiopian eunuch, the first Gentile convert to Christianity, is a lasting reminder for us today. Philip had been one of the seven leaders appointed to serve the church in Jerusalem (Acts 6:1–7). The wave of persecution that began after the stoning of Stephen forced Philip, along with many others, to flee north towards Samaria.

Now, as has been well documented, the Jews and the Samaritans didn't mix. The Samaritans were of Jewish ancestry, but after the Assyrian succession of the Northern Kingdom of Israel in around 725 BC, the Jews from this region were dispersed throughout the Assyrian empire, where they intermarried with people from other conquered states.[105] Consequently, when the exile was over, the Jews who hadn't intermarried considered themselves as a pure remnant and looked down on the Jews from the North. The Samaritans, as they were known, were a not pure bloodline; they had been corrupted by intermarriage and the like.

At the time of Jesus, there was ethnic tension between the Jews from Jerusalem and the Samaritans, such that a Jew travelling north would completely avoid walking through Samaritan villages.[106] When Jews from Jerusalem went north because of the persecution, evangelism among the Samaritans seemed unlikely.

Amazingly the opposite happened. Philip went into Samaria and preached the gospel with great success, and many came to believe (Acts 8:6–8). Soon afterwards, John and Peter joined them. The Spirit was poured out, and fellowship followed (Acts 8:14–25). The disciples had obviously remembered the story Jesus had told about the Good Samaritan (Luke 10:25–37) and understood that it was their responsibility to love the Samaritans as their neighbour. Luke makes the point of including the famous story of Philip and the Ethiopian eunuch (Acts 8:26–40) to show that the gospel was going to Samaria as Jesus predicted. Here the seeds for multiethnic ministry flourished. But notice that, for the gospel message to go beyond Jerusalem into Judea and Samaria and to Africa via the Ethiopian, God established a cross-cultural relationship.

Let's identify a couple of things from the famous story. One day while in Samaria, Philip is told by the Spirit to go south, down the road to Gaza. While on his journey, he meets an Ethiopian eunuch, a high-ranking official in the courts of Queen Candace, who happens to be in charge of the entire treasury. The eunuch happens to be returning from a pilgrimage to Jerusalem and is reading a scroll from Isaiah 53:7. The Spirit tells Philip go over to the chariot and meet him.

This is the heart of all ministry in a multiethnic church – a willingness to build relationships cross-culturally. Upon Philip's querying, the eunuch asks the disciple to explain the meaning of the Isaiah texts and invites Philip into his chariot. Think about what is happening here. This eunuch, regarded as a Gentile, probably went down to Jerusalem for a once-in-a-lifetime pilgrimage to the holy land, probably purchasing a copy of this scroll while there. Because he wasn't Jewish, he would have been made to worship in the Court of the Gentiles, made to worship as part of another congregation.

And, the eunuch's reply to Philip, who has questioned him about whether he understood what he was reading, is telling. 'How can I, unless someone guides me?' (Acts 8:31). He's saying, in essence: 'How can I understand unless a Jew tells me what this means? I want to know who this passage is speaking about, but when I was in Jerusalem none of them wanted to associate with me'. Amazingly, it so happened that the Jew coming across the eunuch's path this day is different from those in Jerusalem. Philip wants to build a relationship with this non-Jewish African. Philip steps into his chariot and shares the gospel with him.

This is a powerful lesson for us. In building a multiethnic church, we must step out and establish friendships and relationships with people from different backgrounds. In fact, it is more important for the church to be concerned more with building relationships than building church programs. Multiethnic communities must have a heart for going directly into the neighbourhood and establishing relationships. I conclude with the words of Michael Frost and Alan Hirsch, who concur with the importance of establishing relationships.

> The missional-incarnational church is well aware of the importance of the web of relationships, friendships, and acquaintances for mission. Christian mission is a relational activity that happens through the conduit of human relations.

The incarnational approach is opposed to the idea of simply developing churches full of people looking for the affirmation of other, like-minded people [or those of the same nationality]. Accepting others, whether Christian or not, is imperative. The stronger a church can build the nets of friendship with other Christians and not-yet-Christians, the greater likelihood of effective mission occurring'.[107]

CHAPTER 9
NURTURING THE ASYLUM

Embracing a multiethnic vision is one thing, but a multiethnic church doesn't just happen. While the last chapter examined the principles for getting the church started, this chapter is about the long-term nurturing of a community made up of people from all nations. Nurturing a multiethnic church is a slow process. As the old expression goes, 'Rome wasn't built in a day'. It requires ongoing commitment to developing the community so that it will continue to thrive and grow.

Some time ago, I sat down with a few men from our church during a men's breakfast. Let me describe the kinds of people I saw fellowshipping together.[108] First, there was John, a former officer in the Australian Navy who had also served thirty years as a constable in the New South Wales Police Force. Second, there was Binh, an immigrant from Vietnam. Binh had previously been a gang leader and drug addict from the streets of Cabramatta. Binh had been invited to attend our service, after which he miraculously gave his heart to the LORD and left his life of crime. Next at the table was Ashane, a former guerrilla fighter with the Tamil Tigers, a militant group operating in Sri Lanka. After escaping Sri Lanka, he fled to the Middle East, where he gave his life to the LORD. Then there was Benjamin, originally from Iraq. In Iraq, Benjamin had served as a soldier in Saddam Husain's army; after escaping, he found himself on a long journey before eventually arriving in Australia and converting. Also present with us was Robert, a lawyer, who came from a strong Italian Catholic background, and Jeffrey, a medical practitioner, who came from a Chinese Buddhist upbringing.

As I looked around that table, I was struck by the amazing combination of people present: a policeman, a gangster, a former militant revolutionary, a soldier, a lawyer, a doctor and a pastor. An Australian, Indian, Sri Lankan, Vietnamese, Italian, Chinese and Iraqi all enjoying breakfast together. We came from different ethnic and religious backgrounds, yet we were eating together at one table, united in Christ. This is just a small sample of people who have joined together in fellowship at Parkside church over the years.

The obvious question that comes to mind is, how do you nurture a community like that? How do you keep it all together? How do you maintain your commitment to God and cultural harmony? With such a vast array of opinions, practices, beliefs, cultural expressions and sheep to feed, how do you appease everybody? When you are a pastor, people expect so much of you and your leaders. Imagine trying to cater for the expectations of over 60 different nationalities. Well, I can tell you, it is not easy. It requires a lot of prayer, a lot of patience and a lot of energy. Above all, you need God's wisdom and God's strength to nurture such diversity. This chapter will examine the distinctives of trying to nourish a multiethnic church through the building of a relational community.

To begin, we must first return to the Scriptures.

PAUL'S LETTER TO A MULTIETHNIC CHURCH

In Acts 18:19—20:38, Luke records Paul's missionary activities in Ephesus. We are told on several occasions that the audience at Ephesus who heard the gospel message came from diverse backgrounds (emphases mine):

> So Paul left them. He took the disciples with him and had discussions daily in the lecture hall of Tyrannus. This went on for two years, so that all the *Jews and Greeks* who lived in the province of Asia heard the word of the Lord (Acts 19:9–10).

> When this became known to the *Jews and Greeks* living in Ephesus, they were all seized with fear, and the name of the Lord Jesus was held in high honour (Acts 19:17).

> I have declared to both *Jews and Greeks* that they must turn to God in repentance and have faith in our Lord Jesus (Acts 20:21).[109]

As such, it shouldn't surprise us that Paul's letter to the Ephesians would have a real multiethnic dimension to it. The city of Ephesus was a wealthy commercial centre in Asia Minor. Its strategic coastal location, harbours and proximity to trade routes made it the ideal providential capital in Roman-occupied Asia Minor.[110] Adjacent to the Mediterranean, Ephesus the city had a diverse religious tradition, particularly with respect to the imperial cult and sorcery.[111] The city was most renowned for the Temple of Artemis (Diana), one of the Seven Wonders of the Ancient World.[112]

We know that Ephesus had a large population of Jews at this time, dating from the century prior to Christ.[113] These Jews were given special privileges by the Romans, including exemptions from military service, freedom to practise religion and permission to send money to the temple in Jerusalem.[114] Consequently, from the very beginning, converts at Ephesus were of both Jewish and Gentile origin. Ephesian Christians were multiethnic. Therefore, when Paul eventually wrote to the Christian community during the early 60s AD,[115] it shouldn't surprise us that the apostle would be considerate of the ethnic parameters prevalent in the church. Paul was concerned with nurturing the faith of these believers, challenging them to live harmoniously.

> Praise be to the God and Father of our LORD Jesus Christ, who has blessed us in the heavenly realms with every spiritual blessing in Christ. For he chose us in him before the creation of the world to be holy and blameless in his sight. In love he predestined us for adoption to sonship through Jesus Christ, in accordance with his pleasure and will – to the praise of his glorious grace, which he has freely given us in the One he loves. In him we have redemption through his blood, the forgiveness of sins, in accordance with the riches of God's grace that he lavished on us. With all wisdom and understanding, he made known to us the mystery of his will according to his good pleasure, which he purposed in Christ, to be put into effect when the times reach their fulfilment – to bring unity to all things in heaven and on earth under Christ (Eph 1:3–10).

The mystery is clear for all to see: that now, under the new world Christ was bringing about, there is unity for all Jews and Gentiles. We are reconciled to both God and each other. The 'dividing wall of hostility' is pulled down.

> As for you, you were dead in your transgressions and sins ... But because of his great love for us, God, who is rich in mercy, made us alive with Christ even when we were dead in transgressions – it is by grace you have been saved. And God raised us up

with Christ and seated us with him in the heavenly realms in Christ Jesus, in order that in the coming ages he might show the incomparable riches of his grace, expressed in his kindness to us in Christ Jesus. For it is by grace you have been saved, through faith – and this is not from yourselves, it is the gift of God – not by works, so that no one can boast (Eph 2:1–9).

But now in Christ Jesus you who once were far away have been brought near by the blood of Christ. For he himself is our peace, who has made the two groups one and has destroyed the barrier, the dividing wall of hostility, by setting aside in his flesh the law with its commands and regulations. His purpose was to create in himself one new humanity out of the two, thus making peace, and in one body to reconcile both of them to God through the cross, by which he put to death their hostility. This means that all peoples from every culture now have the same access to God. For through him we both have access to the Father by one Spirit (Eph 2:13–17).

In light of this great truth, how did Paul want the church to respond? Firstly, by appreciating the fact that the house of the LORD is one house for all people (2:19–22), and secondly, by effectively living this principle in action (see 4:1–3; 5:1). This letter was about nurturing the faith of the Ephesians so that they could be a multiethnic church.

Let us now devote attention to the key principles for nurturing a multiethnic church.

KEY PRINCIPLES

1. CREATE A SENSE OF BELONGING

> Consequently, you are no longer foreigners and strangers, but fellow citizens with God's people and members of God's family (Eph 2:19).

> For there is no difference between Jew and Gentile – the same Lord is Lord of all and richly blesses all who call on him, for, 'Everyone who calls on the name of the Lord will be saved' (Rom 10:12–13).

Former French President Valery Giscard d'Estaing commented: 'You can't build a society purely on interests; you need a sense of belonging'. As Paul wrote in Galatians 3:28–29, regardless of our ethnicity, gender or wealth, we all belong together. Exclusivity in nationality, gender and socio-economics were revealed in the three-fold liturgical prayer of the pious Jewish male, who during worship would thank God for not making him a Gentile, a slave or female.[116] But Paul makes it clear that we belong together.

This was not the first time Paul had encountered the problem of disunity. In Galatians 2, he refers to an incident that took place at Antioch in which even Peter had been led astray into observing a practice that promoted disunity. In Antioch, these false teachers had tried to create a Jewish-Christian table on one side and a Gentile-Christian table on another when it came to fellowship. Accordingly, Paul's entire argument centres on the fact that God has one family, not two. At the foot of the cross, there are no distinctions between Jew and Gentile, slave and freedman, male and female. All belong to God's family. In the life of the church, this ought to play out in the way we create an environment in which all people groups feel included. We are to worship, walk and work together.

To nurture a multiethnic church, we must realise that it is ultimately up to the Holy Spirit to bring it all together. Graham Hill provides a useful description of diversity in the church: 'The church is remarkably diverse – in giftings, temperaments, cultures, ages, socio-economic backgrounds, political persuasions, and ethnicities. Yet the Spirit unifies the church in all its remarkable diversity, guiding it into worship, mission, and glorification of Christ'.[117]

Everyone in the community, regardless of ethnicity, needs to feel valued and accepted. They must be welcomed as individuals who are truly no longer 'strangers'. All people must be included and involved in the life and decision-making of the church.

2. BUILD ON THE SOLID FOUNDATION OF GOD'S WORD

> Everyone then who hears these words of mine and acts on them will be like a wise man who built his house on rock. The rain fell, the floods came, and the winds blew and beat on that house, but it did not fall, because it had been founded on rock. And everyone who hears these words of mine and does not act on them will be like a foolish man who built his house on sand. The rain fell, and the floods came, and the winds blew and beat against that house, and it fell – and great was its fall! (Matt 7:24–27).

> For no one can lay any foundation other than the one that has been laid; that foundation is Jesus Christ. Now if anyone builds on the foundation with gold, silver, precious stones, wood, hay, straw – the work of each builder will become visible, for the Day will disclose it, because it will be revealed with fire, and the fire will test what sort of work each has done. If what has been built on the foundation survives, the builder will receive a reward. If the work is burned up, the builder will suffer loss; the builder will be saved, but only as through fire (1 Cor 3:11–15).

These Scriptures warn that any church not built on the foundation of Christ, as revealed in the Bible, will not have any eternal validity. The key to the success of any church is the foundation upon which that church is built. Although many nationalities may make up your church, the gospel message communicates the same timeless truths for all peoples. Our church motto, *'Building People for Eternity'*, is a way for our church to articulate our commitment to building a community centred on the word of God. Today, many churches thrive to build unity by appealing to aspects like tradition, popular culture or New Age spiritualism. Although often well-meaning in their endeavours, in accentuating such external things they overshadow the essential nature of Christian doctrine for building up the body of believers. For those churches seeking a multiethnic model, there is already that solid biblical foundation apparent. By following a multiethnic vision for the church, you are communicating God's love for all people, something Scripture repeatedly does.

Challengingly, multiethnic churches, more so than monoethnic churches, will by nature attract greater numbers of individuals from a variety of religious systems and worldviews. In my experience, multiethnic churches attract many individuals who have grown up with exposure to other belief systems. Although some of these individuals might take the radical step of conversion, they are still interacting with close friends and family who are practising alternative beliefs on a daily basis. It is therefore even more important for the church community and individuals to have a solid grounding in Scripture. This is the only effective way to reach out to such individuals and in turn equip them for the task of reaching out to their families and friends. Further, it helps to have individuals who are well-equipped in biblical apologetics and understand how other religious systems operate. This is all part of the church's evangelistic task. We can often forget that Peter's exhortation, 'always be prepared to give an answer to everyone who asks you to give the reason for the hope that you have' (1 Pet 3:15), is given to both the individual and the whole church community.

Another reason why God's word must take precedence (apart from the theological fact that it is God's word to us) is because all cultures practise church differently, bringing different ideas about the way community life ought to be. It can be very easy for people to see their own traditions as the only authentic way of practising church and to disregard other cultures. This problem doesn't feature as prominently in monoethnic communities, where there's typically one way of doing things. In a multiethnic context, people can very easily get upset and become dismissive of a church if it doesn't do things in a way they are accustomed to.

Therefore, belief in Jesus Christ, and following the instructions given by God concerning how a community should function, must always take precedence. The word of God must be the source of all guidance by which your church community orientates its customs, preaching, teachings and mission. The word of God is the only inerrant source; our cultures and our traditions are not.

3. PROMOTE UNITY WITHOUT UNIFORMITY THROUGH THE APPLICATION OF A CHRIST CULTURE AS THE STANDARD

> But our citizenship is in heaven. And we eagerly await a Saviour from there, the LORD Jesus Christ (Phil 3:20).
>
> Make every effort to keep the unity of the Spirit through the bond of peace. There is one body and one Spirit, just as you were called to one hope when you were called, one LORD, one faith, one baptism, one God and Father of all, who is over all and through all and in all (Eph 4:3).

Maintaining unity while not forcing uniformity is difficult. A church cannot operate without a unified culture. Neither can a multiethnic church operate without creating an environment in which different cultures are free to express themselves. The challenge for multiethnic communities is this: how do you effectively integrate new cultures and new styles of worship into the life of the church? How do you effectively incorporate value-adding parts of other cultures into the church experience? And how do you do these things while also maintaining a set of values that unifies the church experience?

The trick is to get the balance right. What you don't want is a 'Corinthian situation', in which people start following separate factions with one saying, 'I follow Paul'; another, 'I follow Apollos'; another, 'I follow Cephas'; still another, 'I follow

Christ' (see 1 Cor 1:10–17). You don't want people believing that their culture is more biblical or superior to the dominant culture they are in.

Though we appreciate and embrace one another's cultures, the most important aspect of being a multiethnic church is following a *Christ culture*. The identity we have is a new identity, shaped not by our individual heritage or culture but by our new spiritual heritage. That heritage comes from heaven. The culture, traditions, beliefs, customs and worldviews we now share are from a Christ culture that supersedes our old beliefs and behaviours. Everybody must be united under this new culture.

Multiethnic churches must be extremely cautious about imposing the dominant culture and forcing others to come under that umbrella. In the past, it was very popular for missionaries attempting to evangelise colonialised communities to impose their own culture on other communities under the mantra of 'Christianity, commerce and civilisation' (David Livingstone).[118] European settlers believed in the supremacy of European culture, and thus the policy of the empire (which was passed on to the church) was to convert the indigenous populations to European culture and mindset, which included Christianity.[119] The church's missionary task was to see not just the adoption of Christianity by the indigenous communities but also their conversion to European ways of life, education, philosophies, commerce, industry, culture, customs, values, politics and laws. In 1792, William Carey, while discussing the commitment of Christians towards evangelism of the newly discovered world including the Americas, India, New Zealand, New Guinea and parts of Africa, made what is by our standards quite a bigoted comment: 'They are in general poor, barbarous, naked pagans, as destitute of civilization as they are of true religion ... capable of knowledge as we are ... they know nothing of the gospel'.[120]

Today, however, through the influence of globalisation, the Christian movement has come to see itself more as the global church, with the call now to global evangelisation of the world. Through the manifestos of the Lausanne Covenant and proponents like Billy Graham we now see our utmost responsibility to 'unite all evangelicals in the common task of the total evangelisation of the world'.[121] We are starting to understand that the Western culture cannot be the only expression of church.

Quoting from part of articles eight and ten of the Lausanne Covenant:

> We rejoice that a new missionary era has dawned. The dominant role of western missions is fast disappearing. God is raising up from the younger churches a great new resource for world evangelization, and is thus demonstrating that the responsibility to evangelise belongs to the whole body of Christ. All churches should therefore be asking God and themselves what they should be doing both to reach their own area and to send missionaries to other parts of the world. A revaluation of our missionary responsibility and role should be continuous. Thus, a growing

partnership of churches will develop and the universal character of Christ's Church will be more clearly exhibited. We also thank God for agencies which labour in Bible translation, theological education, the mass media, Christian literature, evangelism, missions, church renewal and other specialist fields. They too should engage in constant self-examination to evaluate their effectiveness as part of the Church's mission.

The gospel does not presuppose the superiority of any culture to another, but evaluates all cultures according to its own criteria of truth and righteousness, and insists on moral absolutes in every culture. Missions have all too frequently exported with the gospel an alien culture and churches have sometimes been in bondage to culture rather than to Scripture. Christ's evangelists must humbly seek to empty themselves of all but their personal authenticity in order to become the servants of others, and churches must seek to transform and enrich culture, all for the glory of God.[122]

This new way of thinking has implications for the multiethnic church movement. A multiethnic church should not foolishly believe that the culture of the host nation or one specific nation ought to be the supreme culture that pervades all aspects of church life. The goal is to establish an environment in which all people should feel welcome.

At Parkside, our annual International Night is an opportunity for people to experience what it is like when other cultural groups come together in worship. Although we still have our normal worship in English, we have numerous performances spread out across the night, where different cultural groups can present worship items.

But this cannot be just an annual thing; it needs to be practised weekly. The common ways that we've done this has been through engaging people from different ethnic backgrounds to lead worship on the stage and by integrating different musical instruments like African drums into worship services. We also have a rotating roster so that each week a different cultural group runs our cafes. Lastly, and perhaps most importantly (as we shall discuss next chapter), we have endeavoured to involve people from different backgrounds in the daily activities and ministries of the church.

For further reflection, please read Appendices 4 and 5.

4. ENCOURAGE EQUAL PARTICIPATION IN THE LIFE AND MINISTRY OF CHURCH

One of the key precepts of Protestant theology is the notion of the priesthood of all believers. This doctrine spells out the fundamental idea that, whether clergy or laity, we are responsible to play a role in both speech and deed in the spreading of the gospel message. In such a system of ecclesiology, each member of the body is regarded as a *priest*, responsible for enacting and expounding God's will on earth.[123] We in the church continue to take up God's calling to Israel in Exodus 19 to be a holy nation, a royal priesthood.

> Now if you obey me fully and keep my covenant, then out of all nations you will be my treasured possession. Although the whole earth is mine, you will be for me a kingdom of priests and a holy nation (Exod 19:5–6; see 1 Pet 2:9).

This challenge takes on new significance under the new covenant of Christ, because it is no longer the responsibility of solely one people group but of people from many ethnic groups. In one sense, we are called to be a kingdom of priests from all nations. In practical terms, this means that all people, regardless of ethnic background, must be encouraged to be involved in the life and activities of the church.

As we shall discuss in the next chapter, one ethnic group cannot dominate the makeup of those who are actively involved in serving. The church must endeavour to promote heterogeneity in the demographics of all those who serve. Unequal participation occurs when there are imbalances in the ethnic makeup of those who are seen to be serving. Participation means contributing, and we are all called by God to use the gifts he has given us to make a real contribution to the future. Responsibility for church growth and the general running of the church not only lies on the shoulders of those in appointed positions of leadership, but with all members of the church community.

Nevertheless, it remains the responsibility of leadership to nurture a community where people feel inspired to serve and where those who feel passionate about the vision are endorsed and mobilised for impact. This kind of culture can only come when the laity own the vision of the church. When somebody owns something, they feel responsible for its wellbeing. The church is not like a corporation where shareholders, while having a vested interest in the company, are happy to leave the running of the business to those appointed to senior leadership. The church is more like a self-employed proprietor. Such person is personally vested in the success or failure of the business. They cannot afford to be disinterested or leave the daily running of the business to someone else. They must be entrepreneurial and lead the way. Likewise, it remains the responsibility of all church members to be actively involved. (This rarely happens, of course; it is usually ten per cent of people doing ninety per cent of the work.) The laity will only feel motivated when they see the biblical relevancy of what the church is doing and make a personal commitment to be attached to God's work on earth.

We have found it extremely helpful to run what we call *Commitment Sunday* and *Serve in the House.* On our annual *Commitment Sunday,* people formally renew their vow, before God and the congregation, to commit both finances and service to the ministry of the church. When we needed to raise funds for our new premises, we found it effective to place a picture of bricks on the church wall and have people buy a brick space. It was only a simple touch, but it made people own the vision of the church. Our *Serve in the House* is an annual form on which people write down the ministries they would like to serve in during the next calendar year. It is a great tool for planning purposes, but more importantly it encourages new volunteers to come forward.

I believe one of the reasons churches go under is that they aren't spending enough time constantly revisiting the vision. When this happens, members are not motivated to partake in church mission because there are no set goals. The church goes into maintenance mode, new leaders are not developed, and new ministry opportunities are not undertaken. It is equally important for people to understand that participation does not just mean giving up a proportion of one's time to be involved; it also means putting forward other areas of one's life, including finances and prayer. If the church is to be serious about its mission, people, including the leadership team, need to make a financial commitment.

I can remember being overwhelmed many times by people's generosity towards the church's mission, but I want to share a couple of occasions that have really stuck with me. Soon after we launched our building project under the motto, *'Building People for Eternity'*, an elderly man in our congregation asked me if he could donate some money to the church. This man was living a very simple life; he did not appear well-to-do, and it seemed as if he were one of the poorest members of our community. After giving him our bank account details, I noticed that he had started transferring relatively large sums of money across.

Over a period of several days, he transferred over $30,000. I began to wonder where the money was coming from, and I was pastorally concerned, as I didn't want him to be financially overburdening himself. I visited him and asked him about his generosity, questioning if he was sure about what he was doing. His response will always stay with me. He told me that he had only just come to Christ and felt that in his old age he didn't have the physical capacity to participate in church ministry. But he knew that in making a financial investment, his impact would be longstanding, even long after he was gone.

Another time, I went to visit a member of our church at his workplace. We were fundraising, and he asked me how much we had left to raise. I don't remember the exact amount, but it was in the tens of thousands. He gave me an envelope and requested that I opened it only once I got to the office. When I eventually opened the envelope, he had generously given me a cheque for the remaining balance.

God is not restricted by our financial giving, but he wants us to make a strong financial commitment to his work.

> 'Bring the whole tithe into the storehouse, that there may be food in my house. Test me in this,' says the LORD Almighty, 'and see if I will not throw open the floodgates of heaven and pour out so much blessing that there will not be room enough to store it' (Mal 3:10).

It is amazing that the very God who declared that we should not test him permitted Israel to test him in the one area of their giving. And he promised that he would pour open the floodgates. As any faithful church knows, when the members collectively commit to God, whether it is through our time or our resources, God blesses us even more. And he will bless us for our service infinitely more in eternity.

5. DEVELOP A CULTURE OF LOVE AND GRACE

> Be completely humble and gentle; be patient, bearing with one another in love (Eph 4:2).

> 'A new command I give you: Love one another. As I have loved you, so you must love one another. By this everyone will know that you are my disciples, if you love one another' (John 13:34–35).

It makes sense that we should end our principles with three of the key pillars of Christian theology: love, grace and missional living (below).

No one in need of a blood transfusion would ask the surgeon to tell them the nationality of the person who originally donated the blood. You wouldn't ask, 'is that Indian blood or German blood?' Why? Because it doesn't matter. What's important is the blood type, not the nationality of the donor. We must have the same attitude when it comes to the church. Provided the teaching of a church is authentic to the true message of Christ, what matter is the nationality of the members? The blood isn't any more special because the one donating it happens to share the same skin complexion to you. Likewise, a church isn't any more special because people all look the same.

The task at hand to reach people from diverse backgrounds and successfully integrate them into an ethnically diverse community seems daunting. The principle, however, is rather simple. As new people from different backgrounds come into your church – *just love them*. It was just one of the simplest things that Jesus demonstrated time and time again when people approached him. He *just loved them*.

> The people saw them going, and many recognised them and ran there together on foot from all the cities, and got there ahead of them. When Jesus went ashore, He saw a large crowd, and He felt compassion for them because they were like sheep without a shepherd; and He began to teach them many things ... (Mark 6:33–34).

This summary statement, which prefaces Mark's account of the feeding of the five thousand, is a powerful illustration of how Jesus just loved people. The bottom line of Jesus' missional strategy was to *just love people*. He saw them and had compassion for them instinctively. It was a compassion that could only come from the Creator.

We can get bogged down all too quickly in the daily pressures of ministry and dealing with people. Sometimes we need God to remind us that we simply need to love people. It was out of Jesus' compassion that he did ministry. He saw the people's helplessness and chose to 'teach them many things'. His love for them transferred into ministry. No matter who comes into church, from whatever ethnic background, socio-economic status, gender, age, even sexual orientation, we should have compassion on them, because anybody that does not know Jesus is like a 'sheep without a shepherd'. They are lost!

Our compassion is typically extended to people we know and like. Frequently, it also encompasses people who are experiencing difficult times in their life. Our compassion will even extend to people who are living in abject poverty or the downtrodden. There's nothing wrong with these things, as the Bible constantly affirms God's heart for the oppressed and weak; the widows, the orphans and the fatherless require extra love and care. The problem, however, is when such sympathy doesn't result in action. Most people who see a commercial for World Vision feel bad temporarily, but it doesn't result in any action. Imagine if Jesus felt compassionate only temporarily but chose not to do anything. We would all permanently be lost sheep without a shepherd.

Building a culture of love and grace means crafting a compassionate heart. It means putting love into action. When you love someone, your focus is on that person and how you can help them practically and serve them as Christ would, irrespective of that individual's ethnic, economic or social status. The same grace that has been extended to us in Christ must also be extended to all, without discrimination. This message of love must be extended without judgment or condemnation: 'For God did not send his Son into the world to condemn the world, but to save the world through him' (John 3:17).

Part of this challenge will be maintaining a harmonious environment where rich relationships can thrive. In any church there will be misunderstandings, even more so in an environment where different cultures are mixing together. There will be misunderstandings on matters of cultural sensitivity. People won't always get things right. Sometimes people will act in a way or say something that is highly inappropriate, even offensive, to people from other cultures. We must learn to bear with one another, forgive one another and look past minor grievances when they occur.

6. PRACTISE MISSIONAL LIVING

> For you were once darkness, but now you are light in the Lord. Live as children of light, for the fruit of the light consists in all goodness, righteousness and truth and find out what pleases the Lord (Eph 5:8–10).

Multiethnic churches (like all churches) must look towards *the end of the day*. At the end of the day, we must ask what the community is here for. When all is said and done, Christians are not called to 'do church'. Christ didn't say, 'Go forth and make churches with people from all nations'. Instead, he told us to go forth and make *disciples* of people from all nations.

The primary call for Christians is not to do church; it is to do mission. Our primary calling is not about programs; it is about people. People don't get into God's kingdom by attending church or attending church programs. People get into God's kingdom through knowing Jesus personally. Pastors needn't be worried about how many people are attending church; rather, we ought to be concerned about how many people will be in heaven. None of the gospels contain a thesis on how to do church. They contain the story of Jesus.

Therefore, as a multiethnic community, our time cannot be spent predominantly on attractional programs that will bring people from a variety of backgrounds into our church. Instead, it must be about equipping and encouraging the collective body of believers and ministering to the lost. The gospel message is the same message, whether it is preached to South Africans, Chinese, Americans, Pakistanis, Palestinians, Israelis or Sudanese. Nurturing a multiethnic church is not about doing church in an ethnically harmonious way. It is about different ethnicities worshipping together, and together going out to the community in mission. As Mark DeYmaz puts it:

> The intended outcome of establishing a multiethnic church is not unity for unity's sake. Rather, it is to turn the power and pleasure of God – uniquely expressed in a church where diverse people 'are being built together to become a dwelling in which God lives by his spirit' (Eph 2:22) – outward in order to bless the city, lead people to Christ, encourage

the greater body, and fulfil the Great Commission (Matt 28:19–20).[124]

As a pastor of a multiethnic church for over 30 years, I am no longer concerned about the ethnic diversity of people attending our church. My paramount concern is the eternal destiny of people, for whom Christ was crucified. It is my desire that the 'multiethnic church model' be a norm for all churches as we seek to faithfully live out Christ's command to make disciples of all nations.

CHAPTER 10
LEADING THE ASYLUM

We often hear it said that attitude reflects leadership. The starting point for transforming a monoethnic church into a multiethnic one is at the top. A monoethnic church will remain monoethnic while the leadership is monoethnic. Whenever a new person walks into your church and sees diversity in God's asylum, he or she must also see diversity in the leadership – among the pastors, the deacons, the Sunday school teachers, café workers, greeters, ushers, band, everybody. The most obvious reason that newcomers who are seeking a multiethnic church will not stay in your church is if they do not believe that you've made enough of an attempt to bridge the ethnic gap.[125] That's why Mark DeYmaz labels the pledge to empower diverse leadership as the 'put your money where your mouth is commitment'![126]

A multiethnic leadership team is one in which no one ethnicity comprises the majority composition of those who serve, and instead, leaders from all backgrounds are empowered and encouraged to participate in all offices of church life.

Discovering new leaders is an overwhelming challenge; discovering multiethnic leaders is even more so. As Rodney Woo writes, 'Whatever leadership dynamics and difficulties a homogenous church may encounter, these seem to multiply exponentially with the convergence of several races and cultures'.[127]

In the wider sense, we are all called to be leaders. It is a component of being salt and light to the world, as Jesus commanded (Matt 5:13–16). Nonetheless, there are a group within the body of Christ who are specifically gifted for such a calling (see 1 Cor 12:28). Such people tend to be those appointed in formal positions within the church, like pastors, deacons, elders and ministry leaders. As Charles Wagner notes, these formal leaders possess gifting in both leadership and administration (Rom 12:8; 1 Cor 12:28).[128] He defines these two gifts in the following way:

> Leadership: The gift of leadership is the special ability that God gives to certain members of the Body of Christ to set goals in accordance with God's purpose for the future and to communicate these goals to others in such a way that they voluntarily and harmoniously work together to accomplish those goals for the glory of God.

> Administration: The gift of administration is the special ability that God gives to certain members of the Body of Christ to understand clearly the immediate and long-range goals of a particular unit of the Body of Christ and to devise and execute effective plans for the accomplishment of those goals.[129]

According to Jesus, all leaders must be servants: 'Instead, whoever wants to become great among you must be your servant' (Matt 20:26).

Today, the servant metaphor has become the most influential image shaping Christian perspectives on leadership. Servant leadership was popularised by Robert Greenleaf in the 1970s,[130] and much has been written about it since. Greenleaf wrote:

> The servant-leader is servant first ... Becoming a servant-leader begins with the natural feeling that one wants to serve, to serve first. Then conscious choice brings one to aspire to lead. That person is sharply different from one who is leader first ... The difference manifests itself in the care taken by the servant first to make sure that other people's highest priority needs are being served.[131]

Graham Hill defines servant leadership, or 'servantship', as follows: 'Servantship is essentially about following our LORD Jesus Christ, the servant LORD, and his mission – it is a life of discipleship to him, patterned after his self-emptying, humility, sacrifice, love, values, and mission'.[132] Similarly,

Aubrey Malphurs states that 'Christian leader are servants with the credibility and capacity to influence people in a particular context to pursue their God-given direction'.[133]

The concept is found throughout Scripture (see Matt 20:28; Mark 10:42–44; Phil 2:5–11; Isa 42:1–4; 49:1–7; 50:4–11; 52:13—53:12).[134] The Greek term *diakonos*, often translated 'minister' or 'deacon', literally means 'servant'.[135] Jesus described himself as a servant (Matt 20:28), and displayed such humility through his actions (John 13:1–17; Phil 2:6–9). Jesus was the suffering servant promised in the Old Testament, through whose suffering brought restoration between God, Israel and the nations. (Isa 42:4–6; 49:5, 8; 49:6; 53).[136] Subsequently, Jesus called on his disciples to have the same leadership style (Mark 10:43, Luke 22:24–27). As John MacArthur notes, authentic leadership is 'service, sacrifice and selflessness'.[137] As the popular leadership mantra goes, 'People don't care how much you know until they know how much you care'.[138]

Let's take a deeper look at the characteristics displayed in servant leadership, particularly as they apply to the multiethnic context.

CHARACTERISTICS OF A MULTIETHNIC CHURCH LEADER

> But select capable men from all the people – men who fear God ... (Exod 18:21).

1. PASSION FOR MULTIETHNIC MINISTRY

> Then I heard the voice of the LORD saying, 'Whom shall I send? And who will go for us?' And I said, 'Here am I. Send me!' (Isa 6:8)

> Woe to me if I do not preach the gospel! (1 Cor 9:16b).

Passion is a powerful instrument for serving God. Ronnie Floyd once said, 'I believe that when God calls you, he always gives you an insatiable passion to make a difference with your life'.[139] Passion is one of the most important qualities we must look for in potential leaders. Passion can only come from one's own personal relationship with God and the burning desire to see people come to a personal belief in Jesus Christ. Scottish evangelist Oswald Chambers, who died while spreading the gospel to troops in World War I, commented, 'The main thing about Christianity is not the work we do but the relationship we maintain and the atmosphere produced by that relationship'.[140] A strong relationship with God produces a contagious atmosphere around a believer, encouraging them to share their passion with others.

This issue was evident in the life of Peter, when Jesus asked him 'Do you love me?' then told him, 'Then feed my lambs'. Jesus was really saying to Peter, 'If you are passionate about me, then do the work I've called you to'. Dave Earley and Ben Gutierrez identify the challenge like this, 'The challenge is to so develop our hearts that we have passion for Jesus and compassion for others'.[141]

If a leader is passionate about Jesus, then his compassion for others should also be non-discriminatory. How can a leader be passionate about preaching the gospel, just as Christ commanded in his Great Commission, yet be discriminatory in the ethnicity of those to whom they preach the gospel? What sets apart a multiethnic leader is the calling that God gives to specifically work with people from all different backgrounds. Almost two hundred different ethnicities are represented in the demographics of our community, and it is the mission of Parkside Church to see people from all these ethnicities coming to faith in Christ and worshipping together as one united community.

Without passion, ministry will become monotonous and wearisome. A vision cannot be achieved unless a passionate team of people unite. Neither will a vision be achieved with divided passions. At Parkside, we will not put anyone into a position of leadership unless they first demonstrate a commitment to the multiethnic vision. Can you imagine if, after Moses had passed away, Joshua his successor suddenly said, 'Sorry LORD, my passion is not to see us inherit the Promised Land – I want us to go back to Egypt'? Such a thought is foolish. If that was Joshua's passion, then he would never have been appointed as Moses' successor. It is vital to have leaders whose passion is directed in the right place.

Some people are passionate but not hard-working. You know the type. They love talking about their passion and how they want to see transformation, but they can never make their passion a reality. Sometimes these people lack the discipline; other times they just talk a big game. Either way, these sorts of leaders can be inspirational yet dangerous, because they promise the world but deliver nothing. There have been times in ministry when we've ventured out on new projects and commissioned a new leader who displays all the signs, but that person never lives up to the hype, leaving the church discouraged and forced to pick up the broken pieces.

Passion cuts to the heart. Truly, passion for God will be the only thing that gets a leader through the stormy seasons in ministry. What's more, passionate people draw others to them. Why do we gravitate toward sermons that are delivered with passion? It is because we cannot help but be inspired by the energy and the power of delivery, as the preacher shares his or her convictions. Passionate leaders are infectious. The energy and enthusiasm produced by passion is transferrable. This is the quality all multiethnic leaders need.

2. BIBLICAL UNDERSTANDING OF GOD'S MISSION

A multiethnic leader not only understands the biblical and theological foundations for multiethnic ministry, but they must acknowledge their own part in God's mission and be prepared to tackle the frustration that can come with intentionally ministering among multiple ethnicities. Having a team committed to evangelising different ethnic groups is critical to the growth of a multiethnic church. Transferred growth from other churches is not the most ideal way of growing God's kingdom to begin with. Additionally, most people who leave a homogenous church for whatever reason will usually try finding another monoethnic one. Therefore, leaders in a multiethnic church must have a strong commitment to reaching people from all nations; otherwise the church will struggle to maintain any long-term growth.

At Parkside, over the years, our growth has predominantly come from brand new believers, who have either never stepped foot in a church or who have fallen away from church life. In our early days, before the days of baptismal pools, we baptised 27 such people in one service.

In your ministry teams, develop a core group of individuals who are deeply committed to God's word and have a strong theology of mission. We are to baptise individuals from all nations in 'the name of the Father and of the Son and of the Holy Spirit,' and teach disciples from all nations 'to obey everything [Jesus has] commanded you ...'.

3. EXPERIENCE WITH MULTIPLE ETHNICITIES

> I have become all things to all people so that by all possible means I might save some (1 Cor 9:22).

One of the most desirable qualities in a multiethnic church is leaders who've had exposure with multiple ethnicities. Incarnate leadership is the type of leadership style that exposes a person directly to a specific ethnic context. The purpose is for them to become personally acquainted with that culture, through experience, in order that they may become a more effective leader. You cannot be an effective leader unless you yourself can relate to the common experience and worldviews of the people you are ministering to.

For Jesus to be most effective as a leader, he had to become flesh and take up residency among the people he was ministering to (John 1:14). Jesus became human and took part in the universal human story. According to Michael Frost and Alan Hirsch, Jesus' incarnation is the very 'prism' by which we understand the missional leader.[142]

The theological foundations for this style of leadership ministry arise from doctrines of Christology and the incarnation, found in John 1:1–18, specifically verse 14, which states, 'The Word became flesh and made his dwelling among us'.[143] The incarnation literally means Immanuel, 'God with us'.[144] It is through the incarnation that we get a truly definitive view of God's character. God is prepared to get his hands dirty. As such, the multiethnic leader must take his or her cue from the incarnation; as Jesus served humanity by entering in, so must his followers.[145]

What's more, the multiethnic leader is prepared to contextualise the gospel and church practices to fit the cultural context, without compromising biblical truths. Contextualisation involves 'understanding the language, longings, lifestyle patterns, and worldview of the host community and adjusting our practices accordingly without compromising the gospel'.[146]

Alan Roxburgh has described this approach as being present in the neighbourhood.[147] It requires leaders to live among people in the communities, just as Jesus did, to love them, fellowship with them, understand them and promote the gospel in action and deed. In this view, leadership is about going out rather than drawing non-believers in.

God naturally has no limitations to his knowledge of all people groups and different cultures, but we unfortunately in our limited capacity do not share that same advantage. Therefore, multiethnic ministries require leaders who have had as much exposure as possible to a variety of people groups and have the ability to engage and develop relationships with people from different backgrounds. Such exposure is what made the Apostle Paul such a pragmatic leader.

In Acts 17, we see Paul was prepared to enter the culture and use Athenian symbols and spirituality to introduce the gospel to people who were not of the same cultural background as he was. Think about the three different cultures Paul had exposure to. He was of Jewish ethnicity, a Roman citizen and clearly educated in Hellenised (Greek) schools of philosophy. One verse in Scripture best captures Paul's cultural competency: 'For God, who said, "Let light shine out of darkness," made his light shine in our hearts to give us the light of the knowledge of God's glory displayed in the face of Christ' (2 Cor 4:7). Three different images: light, knowledge, glory! The Jews well understood the metaphor of light with respect to God (see Gen 1:3–4; Isa 9:2). Greeks looked for knowledge and wisdom (see

1 Cor 1:22). The Roman Empire wanted glory (see Rom 8:30). In one verse, Paul highlights his experience with all three groups by using the metaphors they understood.

Imagine having leaders who understand the inner workings of different cultures in your team. You too can have the same impact!

4. A TEACHABLE SPIRIT

> Give instruction to a wise man, and he will be still wiser; teach a righteous man, and he will increase in learning (Prov 9:9).

> And he said, 'How can I, unless someone guides me?' And he invited Philip to come up and sit with him ... (Acts 8:31).

One of the problems I've encountered throughout my ministry experience is that there are relatively few books or resources available about multiethnic ministry. Nor are there existing models around the world of multiethnic churches. What's more, most of the material we use in Australia, whether books on leadership, theology, church practice, mission, counselling or anything else, comes from a typically Western perspective. There isn't much readily available material from non-Western authors.

With respect to mission, Graham Hill writes,

> The missional conversation in Western contexts continues to be dominated by white (Caucasian),

> middle-class, Euro-American, tertiary educated males ... the following voices are mostly absent or, at least, get very little attention: females, minority groups, the economically disadvantaged, and missional leaders from the Majority World.[148]

This factor can be difficult, especially when seeking to understand other cultures' expectations and practice of church. There are few resources to consult. More often than not, this type of training can only come on the job; it is a type of situation-based learning. Only by spending time with people from other ethnic backgrounds and being open to learning from them can you mature as a leader.

As any couple in a biracial relationship can attest, it takes a lot of hard work to understand each other's culture, expectations, upbringing and family. This becomes even more complex in multiracial group scenarios. Different cultures have different priorities, and they expect different things from their leaders. For instance, in many Eastern cultures, respect for elders is the utmost cultural duty. They will address elders and people in leadership using titles of respect and even greet them by bowing. In Western cultures, this is rarely the case. The individualism of Western cultures is very challenging for those from Eastern cultures. Any leader who does ministry among different ethnic groups must grow an aptitude for managing these kinds of differing cultural expectations.

That said, the only real solution for any leader who wants to have a thriving ministry among diverse ethnicities is to have a teachable spirit. Leaders must be willing not only to learn new things from other cultures but also to try new models and experiment with unverified methods. A lot of what you may try will be uncharted and trailblazing. That's okay. The Christian life is about being taught by God. The lessons that you learn through experience, both positive and negative, must be used to shape the future. In fact, to be a disciple means to be a 'learner' or 'student'.[149] The most effective leaders are those who exegete their environment and adopt the most appropriate leadership style and practices to suit the context. This requires leaders who are by nature flexible and willing to adjust their usual styles and philosophies. The worst mistake you can make is to be intellectually convinced that a multiethnic church is the God-ordained way to go but then not be willing to make changes as you learn from new cultures.

5. RESPECT FOR CULTURAL DIFFERENCES

> Show proper respect to everyone, love the family of believers, fear God, honour the emperor (1 Pet 2:17).

Respecting ethnic differences involves identifying and appreciating the characteristics (values, beliefs, customs, traditions, family dynamics, expectations, ways of thinking) of your own cultural identity and that of others. It includes acknowledging both commonalities and differences between community groups with the intention of engaging in church life in a harmonious manner. Robust intercultural relationships can only be achieved through mutual respect. Respect is founded on the recognition that every person has their own unique relationship with God and can be used by him to advance the kingdom. Respecting other cultures does not include upholding one cultural group's expressions and style of church above another's. Instead, it means integrating different experiences. I want to illustrate how respect plays out in the life of the church by extrapolating two principles from one of the most widely cited passages on leadership qualities in the Bible:

> Here is a trustworthy saying: Whoever aspires to be an overseer desires a noble task. Now the overseer is to be above reproach, faithful to his wife, temperate, self-controlled, respectable, hospitable, able to teach, not given to drunkenness, not violent but gentle, not quarrelsome, not a lover of money. He must manage his own family well and see that his children obey him, and he must do so in a manner worthy of full respect. (If anyone does not know how to manage his own family, how can he take care of God's church?) He must not be a recent convert, or he may become conceited and fall under the same judgment as the devil. He must also have a good reputation with outsiders, so that he will not fall into disgrace and into the devil's trap.

> In the same way, deacons are to be worthy of respect, sincere, not indulging in much wine, and not pursuing dishonest gain. They must keep hold of the deep truths of the faith with a clear conscience. They must first be tested; and then if there is nothing against them, let them serve as deacons.
>
> In the same way, the women are to be worthy of respect, not malicious talkers but temperate and trustworthy in everything.
>
> A deacon must be faithful to his wife and must manage his children and his household well. Those who have served well gain an excellent standing and great assurance in their faith in Christ Jesus (1Tim 3:1–13).

In current church life, we tend to recognise two forms of leaders: volunteers or lay leaders, and those who are vocationally called to lead in churches. The qualities listed here are qualities all leaders must exhibit. For good reason, Paul uses the Greek word *dei* (translated in verse 2 as 'is to be'), to indicate that these qualities are not suggestions; they are binding.

From this passage, let's highlight two qualities essential for a multiethnic leader which imply respect for others.

1. Being 'above reproach'. This means a leader must be morally vigilant and accountable. While this does not imply perfection, it does imply a person who avoids situations and habits that would likely bring them under criticism.[150]

A multiethnic leader must respect other cultures by being especially vigilant about matters of cultural sensitivity. What may seem like nothing or normal behaviour to some people can be extremely culturally offensive to others. Things like alcohol or male-to-female touching, although socially acceptable in Western cultures, are not conventional in other cultures. In most churches in Australia, it is nothing to place your Bibles on the floor, write in them or leave them lying around, but for many people from other cultures, walking in and seeing a Bible on the floor would be very off-putting; they would think that you show absolutely no respect for your holy book. Likewise, in some cultures men and women sit separately in church gatherings. Leaders must be above reproach, knowledgeable and respectful of such cultural expectations and differences.

In a world where much more of our behaviour is accessible to the public eye, especially through social media, church leaders must be very wary of how their behaviour will be perceived by the church. The only way around this is if at the start of one's tenure and progressively throughout, the senior leadership makes every attempt to teach and educate all leaders about the various cultural expectations certain groups have. Train others to know what types of behaviours are acceptable to some but considered discourteous to others. Avoid trying to superimpose Western values on every single member of the congregations by expecting them to conform. Instead, be respectful of other cultures and be prepared to modify your behaviour accordingly.

Admittedly, much of what you'll learn and apply will happen on the go. How can we discern which cultural sensitivities to preference in the face of different behaviours and tolerances? Consider the Apostle Paul's example:

> Be careful, however, that the exercise of your rights does not become a stumbling block to the weak (1 Cor 8:9).
>
> Accept the one whose faith is weak, without quarrelling over disputable matters. One person's faith allows them to eat anything, but another, whose faith is weak, eats only vegetables. The one who eats everything must not treat with contempt the one who does not, and the one who does not eat everything must not judge the one who does, for God has accepted them (Rom 14:1–3).

Several times throughout the New Testament, Paul addresses matters and behaviours that are permissible for some but not permissible for others. Quite often, as is the case in both these passages, it had to do with something as simple and as complex as food. That will often be the case in your church. It may seem like something only minor, but grey issues in diverse churches, if not handled properly, turn into major items.

On one occasion I had to request a gentleman not to greet female members of the church with a kiss on the cheek because it was causing offence to another congregation member. The offended was from a Middle Eastern context where that sort of behaviour is not acceptable. Although in Western culture that sort of behaviour may be considered acceptable, you can understand where someone else might take offence. In this case, the Middle Eastern man was distressed in seeing his wife greeted in such a manner. Believe me, these sorts of cultural differences seem innocent enough, but they have the potential to eventuate in major problems if not handled appropriately. The temptation can be to side with the more conservative or offended culture. However, you then risk dismissing or offending the more casual or liberal cultures. In this particular case, I sat down with both the offender and the offended and helped them to understand the difference in cultures without siding with either one. The outcome was positive as now they understood the cultural difference and were able to continue fellowship with one another in the church.

Paul's solution isn't to play mediator and establish rules and regulations for every minor matter of disagreement. Instead he wants the overarching principle of love to be the arbitrating guidelines in grey areas. In this scenario, the offender's response should not be to tell his fellow brother to get over it and embrace the fact that here in Australia kissing someone else's wife as a greeting is acceptable. Rather, he should forego what is culturally acceptable for him in order not to offend a brother. Respecting cultural differences means embracing the best of both worlds. There are cultural blind spots in all ethnicities; together we can help make others see things in a new light.

However, respect is always a two-way street. Without ever compromising biblical values, we must respect the host culture in which we live. In the same way that we desire to respect the values of other cultures, those coming from different ethnic backgrounds must show a respect and willingness to integrate into the culture they live in. They cannot simply impose their own minority culture and disregard the values of the land. This sort of mutual attentiveness is perfectly in keeping with how the Apostle Paul sought to use his freedoms.

> Though I am free and belong to no one, I have made myself a slave to everyone, to win as many as possible. To the Jews I became like a Jew, to win the Jews. To those under the law I became like one under the law (though I myself am not under the law), so as to win those under the law. To those not having the law I became like one not having the law (though I am not free from God's law but am under Christ's law), so as to win those not having the law. To the weak I became weak, to win the weak. I have become all things to all people so that by all possible means I might save some. I do all this for the sake of the gospel, that I may share in its blessings (1 Cor 9:19–23).

We must all have a mutual respect for each other's cultures for the sake of the gospel, so that we can share in the blessings of communion with God and one another. It is, of course, impossible for those in leadership to learn everything about all cultures and ethnicities. Nevertheless, in every culture there are key 'non-negotiable' values that are held dear. It is the responsibility of those in leadership to understand and honour these sorts of values insofar as they are able.

2. *Hospitality.* Jesus demonstrated perhaps the most profound case of hospitality in all of Scripture towards Matthew the tax collector (Matt 9:9–13). A similar story is found in Jesus' treatment of the tax collector Zacchaeus (Luke 19:1–10). It is well documented that people of Jesus' day hated the tax collectors. They were regarded as corrupt and reviled for collecting the taxes of the Romans. For a prominent teacher such as Jesus to be seen eating at the house of this 'unclean sinner' was scandalous.[151] We never hear how Matthew felt experiencing Jesus' hospitality, but it must have been like a wave of love piercing his heart, such that it transformed him into an influential follower who would write the Gospel of Matthew.[152] Through Jesus' openess and his desire to share a meal with this tax collector, he gained a disciple – and we gained one of the most important biographies in the history of the world.

Food is often described as the international language. In multiethnic ministry, the best way to get to know different people is to open your house to them. To this day, Savi and I are constantly opening our home to share a meal with people. As previously mentioned, it is one of Parkside's favourite pastimes to have different ethnic groups running our church café each week. This sort of unity becomes especially infectious for new people when visiting the church. When new people see different ethnic groups eating together, it is a great display of unity. *Hospitality equals respect.* You don't willingly open your open to someone you don't respect. When Jesus shared meals with tax collectors, sinners and the socially marginalised, he was willing to say, 'I respect you enough to engage in a meal with you'. We can sometimes miss the importance of sharing a meal in modern times, because life is so fast-paced, and many meals are fast food, eaten on the go. However, in Jesus' day (to which many cultures can still relate) the meal was almost a sacred thing. It was *communion*.

On one occasion, I remember noticing someone new to the church standing by himself and drinking coffee. As I approached him to introduce myself, he accosted me, saying, 'You need to teach your people to be more welcoming. I've been standing here for twenty minutes and nobody has come up and said anything to me'. And you know what? He was right. When I looked around the room, I saw everyone engaging in conversations with the same people they speak to every week. Fortunately, he was already a believer and was just visiting – I believe he already had a home church. But the lesson was a hard one to learn. Our inability to greet him or show hospitality showed a lack of respect for him. It suggested he didn't matter to us. Showing respect for all cultures is a task for the whole church, but it starts with the leadership. Cultural cliques and inhospitality are the worst forms of disrespect in a multiethnic church.

In summary, then, leaders who respect other cultures are above reproach, and they lead by example through their hospitality.

6. COMMITMENT TO A LONG-TERM VISION

Upon arrival at Parkside, Savi and I made a long-term commitment to the church. We could see that the church was primarily in maintenance mode and realised that growth would require a long-term outlook.

Statistics vary regarding the average time a pastor will remain in one church. The best available research puts the length of tenure at three to four years. During any tenure, a pastor is subject to many ups and downs, bringing high levels of stress and frequently leading to burn out. It can be hard for a church to gain any consistent momentum without stability in the pastoral office. An examination of your local church history can be revealing, particularly if you discover that the church has had a history of short-term pastors coming and going.

All churches need long-term stability and direction, but those seeking to be heterogeneous in makeup need particularly steadfast leadership. Multiethnic churches are by nature harder to lead because you are dealing with a diverse array of cultures and worldviews. For this reason, it is important for the leaders to have a long-term commitment in order to see growth sustained. At Parkside, the early years were very difficult; it is only in looking back that we can recognise the consistent growth. In my observation, multiethnic churches where the leaders have made long-term commitments are the ones seeing exponential growth, both in Australia and overseas.

Unlike some of the other characteristics that we've discussed in this section, commitment to a long-term vision is not solely dependent on the individual ministers; the whole church needs to be in it for the long run. Yes, it requires a pledge from the pastor, but it is as much the responsibility of the whole community. The church must embrace the vision, the pastor and his or her family. They must be steadfast and have the vision continually rearticulated. In response, the pastoral team must themselves be devoted to the church and willing to commit to a longer-term stay.

Early on at Parkside we set forth our ten-year vision, which sent a powerful message to the congregation that we wanted the church to go to the next level – and that our intention was to see it through. This kind of intention requires deep knowledge of your calling in the Lord and confirmation that this is where he truly wants you to be. It requires a forbearing spirit that is prepared to deal with heartaches and difficult people and events in the life of the church. In the Bible, the idea of a forbearing spirit – sometimes translated as 'gentleness' (NIV) or 'reasonableness' (ESV) – is found in Philippians 4:5. In that context, it refers to having a noble attitude and persevering with people, even those on the outside who are difficult to get along with.[153] At Parkside, we've enjoyed a blessing that many churches don't experience. We've had long-term stays for most of our pastoral team. At the time of writing this book, Savi and I have been at Parkside for over 25 years. Our associate pastor has been here for almost ten years, while our current youth pastor grew up in the church. We are extremely grateful to God for the stability of our church. I believe this kind of long-term commitment in our leadership team has been one of the key ways God's worked to make us the church of over fifty different nationalities that we are today.

7. PROACTIVE IN TRAINING LEADERS FROM DIVERSE BACKGROUNDS

Multiethnic churches cannot flourish with monoethnic leadership. It is hypocritical to suggest to your congregation that you are a multiethnic church when the leadership of the church doesn't reflect that. If you're predominantly a church made up of one ethnic group and your leadership is the same, you're not going to get anywhere. The implications for those trying to turn a monoethnic church into a multiethnic can be put rather frankly. An all-Chinese church must endeavour to appoint non-Chinese leaders if it wishes to become more diverse. Similarly, a predominantly white-Anglo church must explore options to appoint non-Anglo leaders. And this goes for any monoethnic church. The diversity of your church can only ever go as far as the diversity of those at the top. Evidence of a leader's commitment to a global vision and multiethnic ministry should manifest itself proactively in training a diverse team. Christ-centred leadership, epitomised in servanthood, both values and empowers partnerships.[154] It remains the responsibility of senior leadership to encourage cultural diversity within all ministry teams, involving all *peoples* in worship, care, and service of the world.[155]

It can be challenging to nurture new leaders, even more so where you're trying to attract leaders from a variety of backgrounds. Good leaders don't just show up on your church doorstep. Nor do great leaders arise without mentoring and training. As Bennie Goodwin noted, 'Although potential leaders are born, effective leaders are made'.[156] Consequently, a 'natural model' in which one waits around for potential leaders to step up and fill gaps isn't necessarily going to produce a diverse leadership team. Neither is simply waiting for your church to become more diverse so that your talent pool can increase. Although it is preferable to have home-grown leaders, who already have the ethos of the church seared into their conscience, the process of evolving good leaders requires a more deliberate, intelligent design. It requires recruitment and ongoing development. Sometimes this recruitment is bold and audacious and might seem like you're throwing a cat among the pigeons.

One of the major reasons why the Christian message flourished was Jesus' intentional selection of those to whom he chose to pass the mantle. When we read the Gospels, we notice that Jesus, unlike his rabbi contemporaries, didn't simply wait for a worthy leader to emerge before training them. Rather, Jesus went out and purposely called his leaders (Matt 4:18–22; 9:9–12; 10:2–4; Mark 1:16–20; 2:13–17; 3:16–19; Luke 5:1–11, 27–31; 6:13–16; John 1:35–57). Jesus' selection was not merely limited to the calling of the Twelve, but also included a wider sending out of the seventy-two (see Luke 10:1–23). This action was countercultural, because sophisticated rabbis never went out in search of disciples; they waited for worthy students, the cream of the crop, to emerge. Among the men Jesus selected were a tax collector, a fisherman and a revolutionary – hardly the intelligentsia of Roman society. Those whom Jesus appointed were not people you would have expected. The same can be said for transforming a monoethnic church into a multiethnic one. You need people who don't fit into the common boxes. Perhaps the most noteworthy of these was Paul of Tarsus, who was a Jew, a rabbi, a Roman citizen, a persecutor, a sceptic and a philosopher from Asia Minor.

The challenge in any leadership development process – whether for leaders in paid or volunteer roles – is to identify those individuals who show signs of potential leadership. Once these individuals have emerged, the task then becomes about nurturing that individual's spiritual and natural giftings for service. As Oswald Sanders noted, Christian leadership is about 'a blending of natural and spiritual qualities'.[157]

Proactively training new leaders requires a formal development plan. The following picture illustrates the Leadership Development Process I've tried to maintain at Parkside.

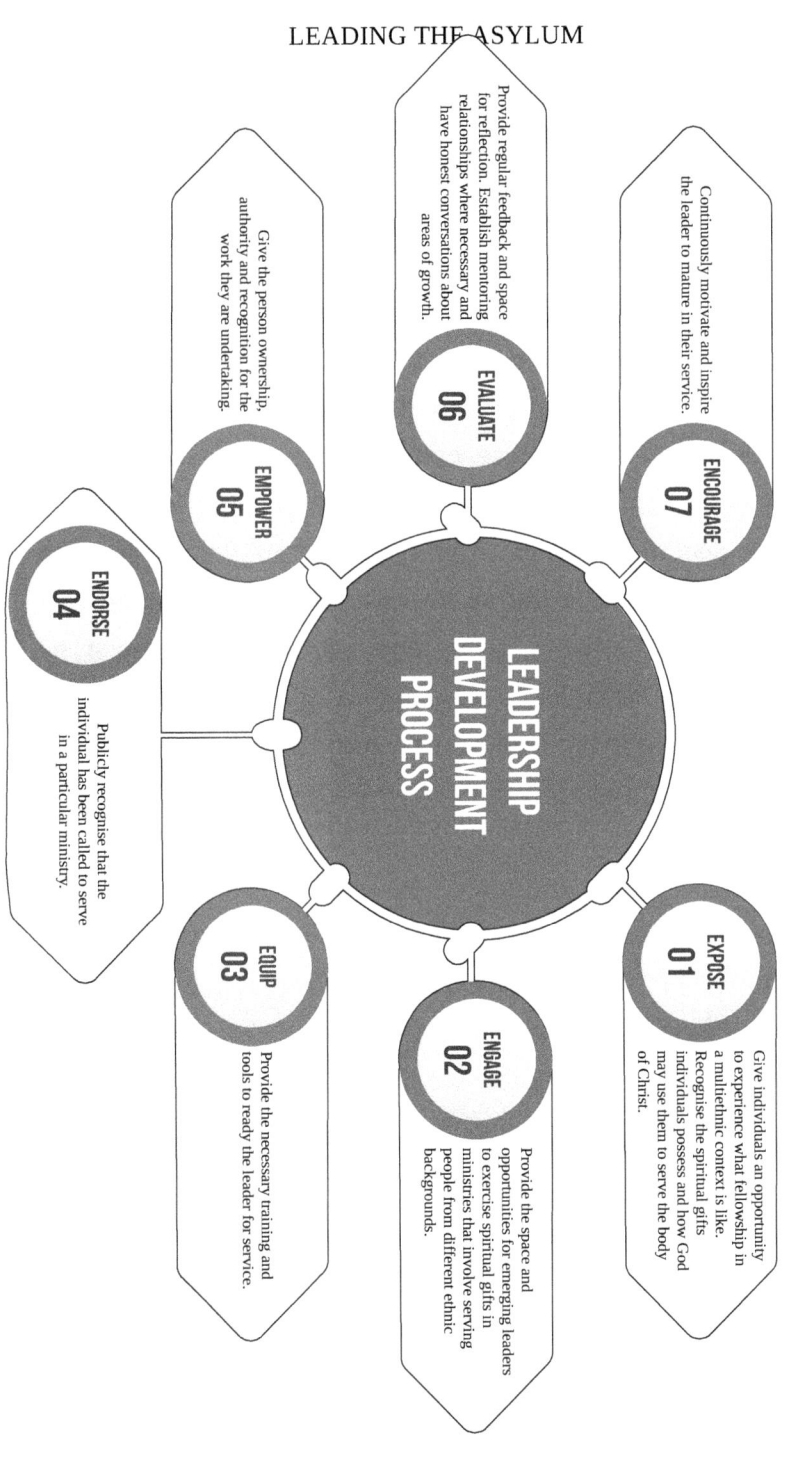

LEADING THE ASYLUM

LEADERSHIP DEVELOPMENT PROCESS

EXPOSE 01 — Give individuals an opportunity to experience what fellowship in a multiethnic context is like. Recognise the spiritual gifts individuals possess and how God may use them to serve the body of Christ.

ENGAGE 02 — Provide the space and opportunities for emerging leaders to exercise spiritual gifts in ministries that involve serving people from different ethnic backgrounds.

EQUIP 03 — Provide the necessary training and tools to ready the leader for service.

ENDORSE 04 — Publicly recognise that the individual has been called to serve in a particular ministry.

EMPOWER 05 — Give the person ownership, authority and recognition for the work they are undertaking.

EVALUATE 06 — Provide regular feedback and space for reflection. Establish mentoring relationships where necessary and have honest conversations about areas of growth.

ENCOURAGE 07 — Continuously motivate and inspire the leader to mature in their service.

A key consideration when developing leaders for the multiethnic context is understanding the range of leadership styles at work.[158] Some cultures are autocratic by nature. These sorts of cultures prefer top-down administration, are typically ethos-centred and bureaucratic by nature, and value the authority of an eldership who impose direction and vision. Very autocratic leadership styles are typically less prone to doing the things listed in the seven E's opposite. In these cultures, it can be difficult for younger leaders to take charge and provoke change. At the other end of the spectrum, typical Anglo cultures are democratic and more resistant to authoritative leadership styles. The authority of elders doesn't always go a long way. A leader must be non-controlling, flexible, group-centred and collaborative. In these systems, younger leaders are more likely to be given an opportunity to engage in ministry without as much imposition from the top.

Whatever leadership style your church is accustomed to, maintaining a good development process that is favourable to attracting leaders from diverse backgrounds may require you to show some flexibility, one way or the other.

These seven principles are foundational when forming leaders who can last the distance in multiethnic ministry. To explore a few other aspects of leadership in a diverse church, turn to Appendices 6–8.

With this chapter, we mark the end of the asylum voyage. Our asylum seekers have journeyed far in their vessel to explore the biblical mandate for multiethnic ministry and the practical questions relating to building and nurturing a church with people from all ethnic backgrounds.

Valuable though this discussion has been, my true desire is to see the conversation about multiethnic churches end as quickly as it has begun. Churches that are made up of people from all ethnic backgrounds who worship, serve and do community together should be the typical church. Multiethnic churches should be the norm. This is God's vision for the church. Today God is taking his gospel all across the world and people from all nations, tribes and tongues are being transformed as they receive salvation through God's grace and the forgiveness and victory that come only from Christ's sacrificial death and triumphal resurrection.

I pray that all who have read this book have been refreshed as well as challenged. And, with all asylum seekers, we pray that which has been the prayer of the church for the past two millennia: *Come,* LORD *Jesus.*

> After this I looked, and there before me was a great multitude that no one could count, from every nation, tribe, people and language, standing before the throne and before the Lamb. They were wearing white robes and were holding palm branches in their hands. And they cried out in a loud voice:
>
> 'Salvation belongs to our God,
> who sits on the throne,
> and to the Lamb' (Rev 7:9–10).

QUESTIONS FOR DISCUSSION

1. Why is it important to build a multiethnic church on the foundation of God's word?

2. Is your church ready to embrace God's vision for a multiethnic church? What preparation and/or changes does the church need to undertake in order to start becoming a more multiethnic community?

3. What are the setbacks of a *multiethnic* congregation with a *monoethnic* leadership structure? How important is it to have diversity in all areas of leadership?

4. How can we promote *unity* without *uniformity* in a multiethnic church? How do we *integrate* ethnicities without imposing *assimilation*?

5. How has this book helped your understanding of a multiethnic church? What further questions have arisen out of your reading of this book?

APPENDICES

APPENDIX 1
THE HOMOGENOUS UNIT PRINCIPLE

In all churches, young and old, bridging growth or cross-cultural evangelism needs to be emphasised. Homogenous unit churches that are only evangelising their homogenous unit are not pleasing to God. Disciples must be made of *panta ta ethne*, all the peoples.[159]

As Jurgen Moltmann points out, the principle that tends to undergird our current way of doing church is the 'birds of the feather flock together' mentality.[160] Much of the contemporary understanding of mission comes from the homogenous unit principle (HUP) mission philosophy. The HUP was a missional and evangelistic methodology advocated by Donald McGavran, Peter Wagner and others from the Fuller Seminary School of World Mission in the 1970s.

Donald McGavran (1897–1990), a missiologist and missionary, has made vast and influential contributions to the field of the Church Growth Movement and to understanding the cultural barriers to effective evangelism.[161] McGavran defined a homogenous unit simply as 'a section of society in which all the members have some common characteristics'.[162] More simply, a homogenous unit can be understood as a group of people with common demographics such as ethnicity, age, linguistics and education. As an experienced missiologist, McGavran knew that 'people like to become Christians without crossing racial, linguistic, or class barriers'.[163] With this in mind, McGavran believed that the most effective way for churches to grow would be to minimise 'social dislocation'. He identified through research that homogenous churches tended to grow and replicate faster – a point I don't deny, as heterogeneous churches are much slower to grow. Simply, the HUP posits that 'people are best reached with the gospel in people groups of the same language, customs, cultures, and beliefs'.[164]

Unfortunately, the HUP has been misapplied to church planting and sustaining across the world. In many cases, this ideology has been borrowed by monoethnic church plants as the ideal way for growth. Many church planters have used HUP as the *modus operandi* for growing their church quickly through seeker-sensitive communities and attractional models. They have opted to use the HUP as a means of evangelising, discipling and worshipping in specific cultural contexts.

Mark DeYmaz, a leading proponent of the world multiethnic church movement, has rightfully asked the question of whether the HUP is actually biblical. More importantly, without wanting to denigrate any of the HUP's proponents, he has challenged some of the long-held presumptions of the HUP used by church planters and growers today.[165]

The problem is one of strategy confusion. In an attempt to grow large churches and attract people quickly into the church community through seeker-sensitive ministries, many churches have misapplied the HUP entirely. Donald McGavran did not intend for the HUP to be a church growth strategy or for bringing more believers into the church community; rather, he wanted the HUP to be a missionary strategy, used to remove cultural barriers when reaching unbelievers. In other words, the HUP is an evangelism strategy, not a principle for how to do church. Though the two are connected, McGavran himself addressed his own concerns that the principle could be misapplied and become a way to foster racial segregation within the church. Two letters, which were exchanged in April and May of 1978 between McGavran and the Lutheran religious scholar Martin Marty, prove very telling. McGavran was responding to an article Marty wrote, entitled, 'Is the Homogeneous Unit Principle Christian?'

From McGavran's response, we learn that motivation to reach the three billion unreached people in the world lay at the heart of the HUP. The principle was about adopting a missional strategy that would reduce the barriers of wealth, language and culture that were proving a hindrance to the advancement of the gospel. Examine these six quotes for yourself.

> The HU principle arose facing the three billion who have yet to believe. Tremendous numbers of people are not becoming Christian because of unnecessary barriers (of language, culture, wealth, education, sophistication, imperialistic stance) erected by the advocates.
>
> I suspect that the basic reason you are keeping an open mind toward the principle is that you sense its importance in the propagation of the Gospel. Do, I beg of you, think of it primarily as a missionary and an evangelistic principle.
>
> Remember also, that those who advocate it also advocate full brotherhood. While I was formulating the Homogeneous Unit principle, Mrs. McGavran and I were the only white members of the All Black Second Christian Church of Indianapolis. We have spent more than thirty years living among dark skinned people in India, eating with them, working with them, regarding them in every way as brothers and sisters.
>
> ... There is danger, of course, that congregations (whether established according to the HU principle or not) become exclusive, arrogant, and racist. That danger must be resolutely combated.

> So be assured that Wagner and I and others using the Homogeneous Unit Principle are with you a hundred per cent in your conviction that brotherhood and unity are of the essence. We hope you will be with us a hundred per cent in our conviction that unnecessary obstructions to accepting the Christian Faith be recognized and done away with.[166]

In the past, missiologists like David Bosch have correctly identified that the HUP, if misapplied, can diminish Christian values of diversity and unity. However, now when someone opens their mouth about being culturally relevant or attractional, they are often unfairly accused of devaluing the importance of heterogeneity in the church community, when that's not what they're really saying. On the other side of the coin, some churches claim to be against all forms of attractional ministry yet are still entirely monoracial in makeup. These churches confuse generational heterogeneity (all different ages within the church) and cultural heterogeneity (many cultures within the church).[167] Multiethnic churches need to be heterogeneous in all areas. There must be ethnic diversity as well as gender, age and socio-economic diversity.

It is important to reiterate that I don't believe homogenous churches are racist or that their leaders don't work their hardest to preach the gospel faithfully to as many people as they can. Nor do I believe that a desire to grow a church is wrong; in fact, if your church does not seek to grow the community of believers, then you're not faithfully following Christ's command to make disciples. Nevertheless, our ministries are not measured by the success of how many people enter our doors but rather how faithful we are to presenting God's unfolding reign throughout the world. If we did seek to measure church growth as the number one metric for a successful ministry, then by that definition many of the heroes of the faith like Isaiah and Jeremiah had unsuccessful ministries, because very few people entered their church doors. Furthermore, by this standard most megachurches have produced a more successful ministry than Jesus himself, who did not plant a single church. In fact, it was Christ who made statements like, 'small is the gate and narrow the road that leads to life, and only a few find it' (Matt 7:14). Therefore, if you seek to use the HUP as a means to grow a church quickly, then you're in the wrong business.

One of the failings of the church growth movement is that it can overlook the fact that conversion is a process – in many cases, a long process – that cannot be sped up simply through attractional methods. Further, although removing barriers to conversion is important, the church growth movement can fail to appreciate that there are what I would call both good and bad (or necessary and unnecessary) barriers to conversion. Playing hymns on an organ is a bad or unnecessary gap if the culture doesn't listen to that kind of music. That is a barrier that needs to be removed. But many barriers are necessary.

The gospel is an unavoidable barrier in and of itself. As Paul articulated, 'We preach Christ crucified: a stumbling block to Jews and foolishness to Gentiles' (1 Cor 1:23). There are aspects of the gospel message that are automatically difficult for people to accept. For some, the morals imposed by the Bible are a barrier to conversion. For others, simply telling them that they are sinners in need of a Saviour is a barrier. For an atheist, the philosophical idea of miracles is a barrier. For Muslims, the doctrine of the Trinity and the crucifixion of Jesus is a barrier. For the Hindu or Buddhist, the idea of Jesus as the only path to salvation is a barrier. Nevertheless, these barriers are essential. We can't remove these barriers simply to speed up conversion rates! Expediency should never cause us to abandon God's will. To do otherwise would be to compromise central Christian teaching.

If a diverse congregation is a barrier to conversion for those who would prefer to associate with people who are of the same nationality, then maybe it is a necessary barrier those people need to cross. If Christianity's diversity is a stumbling block for some, then I'd argue it is a good barrier they need to overcome, not a bad barrier the church should remove. When we try to remove fundamental tenets of the faith in order to make the gospel more palatable, then we risk compromising the very point of our message.

Why must the church be a centre for attracting like-minded people from the same cultural background? Isn't the biblical injunction to 'accept one another, then, just as Christ accepted you, in order to bring praise to God' (Rom 15:7)? Doesn't this acceptance include acceptance of each other's ethnic diversity?

With this foundation in mind, Jurgen Moltmann notes, the 'birds of the feather' idea has no place in the life of the church.[168]

Some have tried to tiptoe around the solution by claiming that once a person becomes a believer then the Holy Spirit will transform them to overcome the ethnic barrier. I am inclined to believe that new believers should be challenged to overcome their biases from the start. What's more, such thinking doesn't square with the fact that we still see many monoethnic churches filled with mature believers. The position is bankrupt. Why haven't those mature believers overcome the barrier yet?

Others have tried to argue for homogeneity by citing the 'become all things to all people' principle of Paul. I am not denying that there are times when you need to obey cultural sensitivities (after all, this is one of the greatest challenges of a multiethnic church). For instance, when evangelising among Middle Eastern people, we must acknowledge there are male and female sensitivities that must be adhered to. However, should a person come to faith, I would hope to slowly start breaking down the gender gaps. This is what the process of discipleship is about. It is about Christ transforming the whole person and the whole person's attitude. Remember, what your community looks like speaks volumes about your theology. If you allow people to remain in pre-Christ attitudes, and you orientate your church practice around such, then you are failing the sheep in your flock. The Bible says that 'we demolish arguments and every pretension that sets itself up against the knowledge of God, and we take captive every thought to make it obedient to Christ' (2 Cor 10:5).

It is going to take from this side of eternity till the next to build the church of Christ. DeYmaz helpfully recognises that principles and terms like the HUP and 'church growth' were not coined as marketing terms to articulate the numbers of people who walked through church doors but rather as missionary terms to articulate the advancement of the gospel to unreached areas by cross-cultural methods.[169] Church growth really means kingdom growth, and evangelism is the way to reach the unbeliever and grow the local church. Unfortunately, the HUP has been misinterpreted. For many churches, the HUP *is* a marketing tool.

We must be careful not to view church growth as the primary objective for mission just because it seems most effective. The primary objective of all church life, including mission, is to win people over to Christ. The HUP, if appropriately applied, can be effective as a mission strategy, helping people overcome barriers to becoming a mature believer. After all, even in a multiethnic church we still have homogenous aspects to some ministries. There still remain ministries targeted at youths, at young adults, retirees, men, women and so on, and these all require some level of attractional development. However, in spite of all this, collectively the church remains ethnically diverse. No ministry is solely just about reaching certain people groups. All ministries come under the banner of ethnic diversity. The challenge should be about closing the gap for the non-believer by pointing them to the fact that diversity is one of the best things about the asylum of God.

APPENDIX 2
BARRIERS TO MULTIETHNIC MINISTRY

Whenever a new product, idea or innovation comes out, factors like its significance, price point and target audience can impact how readily it is accepted by a market. How a group of people embraces something new always follows a curve. Below is a copy of Everett Rodgers' Innovation Adoption Curve.[170]

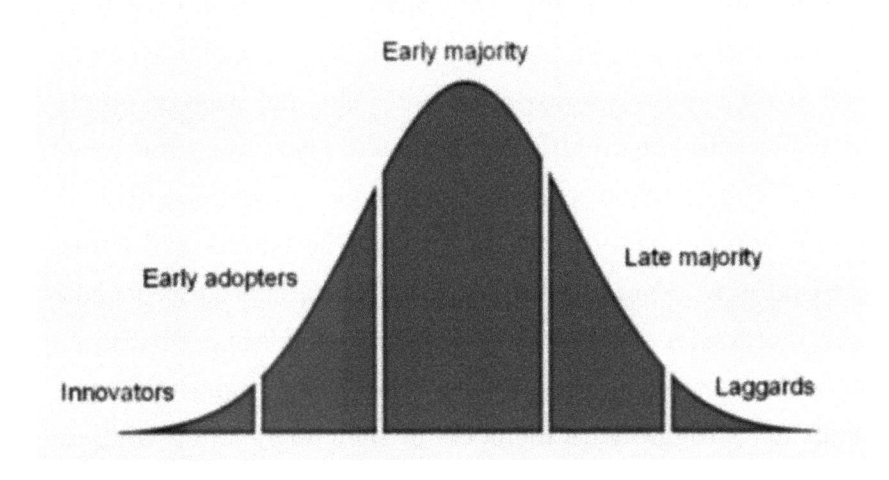

This is as true for ideas, visions and innovations in ministry as it is in the marketplace.

There will be people within your church who will be pragmatic; they'll be right at the forefront of the vision and keen to get things done. At the other end of the spectrum, you'll have those who are more pessimistic and resistant to the changes. But most of your time and attention will be spent focusing on the cluster in the middle.

Keep encouraging the innovators and early adopters without letting them go too far ahead. Use their excitement as positive influence for the majority.

As for the idlers, spend less time and attention on them. Naturally, it is important to address their concerns and not neglect their questions. They, too, are part of God's community; just because someone is in this camp doesn't mean that they don't have the best interests of the church at heart. Moreover, when you are successful at moving them down the other end, they can become some of the greatest advocates. The Apostle Paul, after all, was once a ruthless sceptic. Of course, the opposite can be true; advocates can go down the other end and become voices for disunity. But be mindful that there will always be some down the 'lag' end on whom you can spend hours yet get nowhere.

If you've made it this far through the book – and I trust that God is working in your heart, encouraging you to become more multiracial – then you're probably wondering what to do about that person or people who don't want change. Leaders frequently struggle with members of the congregation who are very comfortable where they are. They like the music, they like the communion table where it is, and they don't want anyone sitting in their pew! These types of people, although I'm sure they mean well, can be a nightmare.

When we ran our multiethnic conference in 2012, we had over thirty Salvation Army leaders come from all across Australia in the hope of making their churches more diverse. Some time later, we received encouraging news that this commitment to diversity was really becoming fruitful, and churches were starting to transition. By their own admission, however, they were having problems trying to integrate some of their Chinese-specific ministries into this new framework.

There will be some people who will want to leave because they no longer feel comfortable with the new direction of the church. Many people prefer being around others of a similar nationality, and this will be their strongest resistance to change. Nevertheless, it is vital that people like this are educated and given a fresh perspective on what the church really is. At Parkside, we invested a lot of attention in the early years to reshaping people's understanding of church. They had to understand that the church was not just a social club but involved commitment. The church is not a place to be comfortable.

In fact, the Christian life is not a comfortable life. As Jesus said, 'Foxes have dens and birds have nests, but the Son of Man has no place to lay his head' (Luke 9:58). And Paul said, 'I have laboured and toiled and have often gone without sleep; I have known hunger and thirst and have often gone without food; I have been cold and naked. Besides everything else, I face daily the pressure of my concern for all the churches' (2 Cor 11:27–28). Neither Jesus nor Paul nor or any other of the apostles had a comfortable church they could go back to once a week.

And even today around the world we see many examples of churches and missionaries facing persecution and heavy oppression. Those individuals who make up the persecuted church aren't part of comfortable churches. Often they meet underground and in secret, their members face rejection from family, imprisonment, torture and more. And yet we dare say today that our church should be comfortable, that we should have comfortable seating and that I can leave this church because it makes me uncomfortable to sit next to someone different from me. Friends, if we want to be comfortable, if we want a comfortable church, then we picked the wrong religion to subscribe to. We picked the wrong God to follow. Why wait till eternity to become comfortable with our heritage? Like it or not, we are a diverse body *now*, and we'd better get used to it.

Comfort is possibly the overarching blocker when it comes to change. Within it, however, I've come across four main barriers to multiethnic ministry.

Ethnocentrism is the belief that one ethnicity or culture is superior to all other cultures. You'll find this in every culture. But this attitude can create arrogance and prejudice towards people from another culture. Helen Richmond and Myong Duk Yang write that the 'greatest hindrance to becoming a multicultural church is the attachment to our own cultures'.[171] These sorts of beliefs often manifest themselves in arrogant opinions that 'our way is right' and 'others can't tell us what to do'. Or, as we can see in the early church with the issue of circumcision, 'they should have to become like us and do church our way and our style'.

Nationalism is the belief that one country is superior to all other countries. It is the attitude that says, 'It is my country and you have no right to be here'. There is nothing wrong with having national pride. As an Australian citizen, I am very proud to be an Australian. I am loyal and committed to this country. But unfortunately, as we explored in chapter 3, some Australians think that only certain kinds of people can call Australia home. For 70 years, Australian immigration law reflected this attitude with the White Australia Policy. I thank God that it was abolished, but unfortunately the mindset of many Australians is yet to change. These attitudes are only fuelled when global events like terrorist attacks help to solidify stereotyped perceptions about different people groups.

Traditionalism is by far the greatest challenge I have had to face in my ministry at Parkside. It seemed to surface in every aspect of our church life, from the style of worship and the type of music to the format of preaching. People in the congregation were constantly reminding me of the old traditions, saying, 'We have always done it this way here'. Some people are full of nostalgia and committed to old traditions: they want to keep Boys' and Girls' Brigades and they still want the old Billy Graham rallies. They don't want the old table in the corner to be moved. They still want to sit in the same pews. They want life to go back to the glory days. This was the problem Jesus had to deal with when it came to the religious group known as the Pharisees. They were constantly criticising him for breaking traditions. The key for people who have this barrier is to recognise that it is their issue to deal with. The progress of the church shouldn't stop just because they're not comfortable with tradition changing. Jesus didn't change his actions to appease the Pharisees. If you give them an inch and say that you'll hold off changing, they'll stop progress completely.

Indifference is the final barrier. Some people are just content and don't really care very much. They are more concerned with their own personal lives. Satan wants people to be apathetic. More than anything else, these people require prayer.

Leaders must be exhorted to speak into these areas. You can't just let them go unnoticed. Further, ministers can't keep preaching to an already existing belief if it is wrong. You will never change anything. Reflect on the story of Elisha and his servant:

> When the servant of the man of God got up and went out early the next morning, an army with horses and chariots had surrounded the city. 'Oh no, my lord! What shall we do?' the servant asked. 'Don't be afraid,' the prophet answered. 'Those who are with us are more than those who are with them'. And Elisha prayed, 'Open his eyes, Lord, so that he may see'. Then the Lord opened the servant's eyes,

and he looked and saw the hills full of horses and
chariots of fire all around Elisha (2 Kgs 6:15–17).

Here Elisha's servant had a barrier preventing him from seeing what God was doing. Elisha's response was to pray that God would open his eyes to seeing things in a new perspective. Educating the congregation is essentially about speaking on behalf of God, so that he can open our eyes to a new way of looking at things: a multiethnic perspective.

APPENDIX 3
LANGUAGE BARRIERS AND MULTIPLE SERVICES

This issue of language is a very difficult one to navigate.

Many churches attempt to solve this by having multiple services. For instance, they may have an Arabic service at 9.00 am and an English service at 10.30 am. In one sense, this is a good impulse, because Christians believe that the Bible can and should be studied in a person's native language. This lies in contrast to the Islamic usage of the Koran, which must be read in Arabic. But there is no such language barrier when it comes to reading the Bible. Today the Bible has been translated into a vast number of the world's languages in order to make it accessible in people's mother tongues, and the work of Bible translation remains an ongoing endeavour.

Nor should there be any language barrier when we gather as a community. We have evidence of this from Scripture:

> Now there were staying in Jerusalem God-fearing Jews from every nation under heaven. When they heard this sound, a crowd came together in bewilderment, because each one heard their own language being spoken. Utterly amazed, they asked: 'Aren't all these who are speaking Galileans? Then how is it that each of us hears them in our native language? Parthians, Medes and Elamites; residents of Mesopotamia, Judea and Cappadocia, Pontus and Asia Phrygia and Pamphylia, Egypt and the parts of Libya near Cyrene; visitors from Rome (both Jews and converts to Judaism); Cretans and Arabs – we hear them declaring the wonders of God in our own tongues!' Amazed and perplexed, they asked one another, 'What does this mean?' (Acts 2:5–12).

It is fascinating that the first thing the Spirit did at Pentecost was to empower the disciples to overcome the language barrier. Over the years. missionaries have been empowered to do the same. These missionaries have spent years learning the language of the most remote communities around the globe. Some have even been able to translate the Scriptures into those languages. The Spirit could have empowered the disciples to go to separate areas and speak different languages directly to new communities, but God wanted a dramatic event to accompany the breaking in of the Spirit. That's what made this event so special; it wasn't just that the disciples suddenly knew a whole lot of other languages. It was special because together they went out proclaiming the gospel message and everybody heard this in a language known to them.

One thing we are very committed at Parkside to is *not* having multiple services in different languages. The reason for this is we want a united church whereby 'Jew and Gentile' can overcome language barriers and worship God together. We can't get that picture of Revelation 7:9 unless we have a communal mindset. This is crucial to understand, Notice what we are told about that great multitude from every language that will be present before the throne:

> They were wearing white robes and were holding palm branches in their hands. And they cried out in a loud voice:
>
> 'Salvation belongs to our God,
> who sits on the throne,
> and to the Lamb' (Rev 7:10).

Did you catch that? They cried together in a loud voice. Not separately. However else we might worship, we must appreciate that our eternal worship of God will be communal. Many churches claim that by offering a variety of services in different languages we are promoting multiculturalism. But how else are we supposed to unite the entire local church community unless we're able to gather *together* weekly for a communal worship of God? Multiple services only serve to divide the church.

We find arguments for the need to separate services based on language to be quite overstated, at least in our context. We've frequently found that people's arguments for multiple services have very little to do with the language barrier at all. Most often, they want separate services for cultural reasons. But let's take a further look at language to see just how much of a barrier it really is.

Collectively, Australians speak over 300 languages at home, but most Australians are bilingual. According to our 2011 national census, over 76.8 per cent of households speak only English at home, while 20.4 per cent of households speak two or more languages. Additionally, at an individual level, 81 per cent of people reported as only speaking English at home. This doesn't mean that they can't speak any other language, but the data suggests that for most people it would be a massive overstatement to suggest that you can't have a collective service because of language barriers.

Like all other nations, Australia recognises the importance of having a national language – English. A national language is essential for unifying a society. We see this as essential for the church as well. Mind you, we're not suggesting what language that should be; it should be whatever language will best unify the entire congregation. At Parkside, it is obviously English. For your church, we would also recommend whatever the national language is. With that said, you could get nations like Denmark in which although, Danish is the official language, to have English speaking congregations would be practical as well, given that large majority of Danes (over 85 per cent) also speak English.

When we look at the other most commonly spoken languages in the 2011 census, we see Mandarin (1.6 per cent), Italian (1.5 per cent), Arabic (1.4 per cent), Cantonese, Greek (1.2 per cent) and Vietnamese (1.1 per cent) featuring in the data. Of course, you can set up churches and service for those pockets. But as we've been trying to illustrate throughout this book, when you do this, you make your church exclusive to people who can only speak those languages.

We should remember that the overwhelming majority of new migrants to a country come with the intention of learning the native language. It is the only feasible thing to do if you're going to live, work and send your children to school in the community. At Parkside, we learned that a collective service not only helps unify the church, but it also helps new migrants learn the language. I can't tell you how often people have come to me to express appreciation for how attending a church with a unifying language has helped them learn the language. This has gone on to help them in their personal life.

Churches are not the only institutions that have to deal with the issue of language barriers; schools, universities and even our Bible colleges must employ a unifying language. Yes, you will have occasional difficulties with the odd person who only speaks the native language from the nation of birth. But that will be the anomaly, and the most effective way to integrate congregational members like that will remain home groups. Nonetheless, the type of culture you really want to advocate is one that values Sunday services and weekly home groups that are made up of people from all different nationalities.

A desire to have a corporate worship service in a common tongue does not devalue multiculturalism, nor does it undervalue the importance of the native languages of our parents, but rather it upholds what true multiculturalism is about. True multiculturalism in the kingdom of God celebrates the things that make us different, while unifying us with the one culture that supersedes our individual national identities – our eternal citizenship.

APPENDIX 4
FOOD SACRIFICED TO IDOLS

A practical example of how a Christ culture was applied to an issue in the early church can be found with respect to the question of food sacrificed to idols. In the formative years of Christianity, concerns arose over the eating of meat which had been sacrificed to idols. It was common in Greco-Roman society for idol meat to be sold in the marketplace. In addition to this there was sacrificial food, which was typically eaten at pagan temples as part of the religious piety of the day.

Because Christianity arose out of a strictly monotheistic Jewish society, concerns were naturally raised over the ethical nature of whether purchasing and eating such meat was an 'unclean' practice. Jewish Christians no doubt perceived this as the wrong thing to do by their culture, while the Gentile Christians didn't think that this was necessarily the wrong thing to do. That said, we probably shouldn't jump to the conclusion that this was only a Jew-versus-Gentile issue. It is fair to speculate that some Gentiles may have been put off by the notion of food that had been sacrificed to idols because it was a reminder of their former life and the former idolatry which they once practised.

Had the churches been monoracial, each community group could have just done their own thing and the issue may not have arisen. However, this was not to be the case. Instead there were multiple cultures that needed to reconcile this issue to promote unity, without forcing conformity on such a grey issue. They needed a Christ culture to be applied as the standard. The council of Jerusalem was satisfied to settle the cultural difference by being diplomatic (see Acts 15:28–29). They were content with saying, 'Let's not overburden anyone; however, just avoid food sacrificed to idols altogether'.

Paul, however, chose to clarify his position on the matter when writing to the Corinthian church. In 1 Corinthians 8:1–11:1 he dealt with the matter of food sacrificed to idols. To simplify (although the issues were bigger than this), in Corinth there were two camps of people: one who felt they had freedom to eat whatever they wanted – going so far as to say that they could even engage in attending the cultic meals that were staged at the temple – and the other who, in forgetting that an idol is nothing but a man-made creation in God's sight, were trying to impose legalistic dietary requirements.[172] Paul's response was to promote unity without forcing uniformity. He corrected those who had gone too far astray and strictly forbade engaging in the temple practice (10:1–22). He then turned to the greyer issue, the question of food sold in the marketplace (10:23—11:1). His verdict challenged those who were being legalistic, affirming that everyday food sold in the marketplace was not unconscionable.

The issue of food sacrificed to idols exposed the need for two cultures to balance different expectations in order to live harmoniously. Paul's response was not to promote one culture's traditions as better than the other. Instead, he wanted them to see that in Christ they had a new culture, and crucial to maintaining harmony in that new culture was an understanding of who God truly is. By understanding who God is, they could then determine how they ought to live as a community. To those who felt their new-found freedom in Christ was a license to engage in temple cuisine, he reminded them of how seriously God treats idolatry. To those who were attempting to be legalistic about food sold in the marketplace, he reminded them that 'The earth is the LORD's and everything in it'.

Therefore, in all matters pertaining to keeping a harmonious church life, follow the biblical exhortation of Paul to the Corinthians:

> So, whether you eat or drink or whatever you do, do it all for the glory of God. Do not cause anyone to stumble, whether Jews, Greeks or the church of God – even as I try to please everyone in every way. For I am not seeking my own good but the good of many, so that they may be saved. Follow my example, as I follow the example of Christ (1 Cor 10:31—11:1).

APPENDIX 5
THE OLD ORGAN OR AFRICAN STYLE?

In 2 Samuel 6, the event is recorded of King David bringing the Ark of the Covenant into Jerusalem. We are told it was quite the festive occasion:

> Wearing a linen ephod, David was dancing before the LORD with all his might, while he and all Israel were bringing up the ark of the LORD with shouts and the sound of trumpets (2 Sam 6:14–15).

Unfortunately, not everybody was pleased with David's merriment.

> As the ark of the LORD was entering the City of David, Michal daughter of Saul watched from a window. And when she saw King David leaping and dancing before the LORD, she despised him in

> her heart ... When David returned home to bless his household, Michal daughter of Saul came out to meet him and said, 'How the king of Israel has distinguished himself today, going around half-naked in full view of the slave girls of his servants as any vulgar fellow would!' (2 Sam 6:16, 20).

Admittedly, there was a lot more going on beneath Michal's anger toward David than just how he expressed himself in worship of the Lord.

However, this incident poses an interesting question. What style should a multiethnic church embrace in its worship?

First, I must acknowledge that it is a tough question. There is the never-ending clash between contemporary worship styles and traditional approaches. Some people want just the organist upfront, some want a choir, others want a livelier concert feel and still others just want to go home! It seems as if there are too many styles to cram into one service. Michael Emerson notes that the church is often viewed as a 'religious mega mall'. There is no one style that everybody loves, and there are always new initiatives your church can try to bring new cultures in. Worshippers go back and forth trying to find what fit their needs best, and churches try to accommodate as many people's preferences as possible. As Emerson argues, 'Nor can all options successfully be offered without ending in chaos'.[173]

Should having to accommodate for over 60 different nationalities complicate things? Absolutely not! Rodney Woo makes the brilliant point with his question, 'Who is the object of our worship?'[174] *God* – not the congregation – is the one to satisfy. Our weekly audience is not over four hundred people from over fifty different nationalities. We're not trying to satisfy the needs and preferences of all these people. These days people have iPod and YouTube and they can listen to their favourite preachers and Christian music anytime. As Woo puts it, at church our audience is 'One'.[175]

The last thing a leader wants to do is tell people of other cultural groups how they should worship God. It will be important to expand the horizons of your worship to include elements of other cultures, particularly those you are trying to reach. Do not limit yourself to a worship style that identifies with only one ethnic group. Remember that incorporating other racial expressions into your band informs a new visitor to your church that their culture matters in the eternal worship of God.

However, while introducing and assimilating different worship styles is important, remember first that the reason for doing it is not because without it your church won't attract that person who is seeking a distinctive style. It is done because you wish to incorporate a new expression into your worship of God. Music is a heart expression of worship, and everybody has their own way of doing it.[176] As Kathy Black notes, harmony is paramount to the European-American way of singing.[177] Emerson asserts that white culture stresses melody; black culture prioritises rhythm and groove.[178] Some people groups, as is common to the African style, want to be expressive in their body movements, clapping and dancing as part of worship. Others need to stand still in the pew and sing off a hymn sheet.[179] But, as Woo emphasises, 'God's multiracial choir singing in harmony announces to the world the harmony that He has brought to the fragmented races in the body of Christ ... In multiracial worship, the church gives the world an opportunity to see the glory of God as reconciled humanity sings in harmony'.[180]

Other aspects of Sunday gatherings raise similar questions. Take the issue of preaching. For some churches, the pulpit is a sacred space from which the preacher conveys a sense of authority and exhorts from the word. Some prefer a preacher who paces back and forth and is dynamic. Others prefer a short homily. George Yancey cites research that suggests service times also vary among different cultural groups. For predominantly white churches, it is just over an hour; for black churches, it is an hour 45 minutes. At Parkside, like multiethnic churches in general, worship times are about 80–90 minutes.[181] Service start times and the adaptability of services is another important question. Some cultures, particularly in the West, require stringent start times; for others, the service starts whenever the Spirit is moving and can last the entire day.

There is no easy solution, nor should we expect there to be. Remember the first commandment, 'Love the Lord your God with all your heart and with all your soul and with all your mind and with all your strength' (Mark 12:30). The key way to understand this is that each person is to love the Lord within the capacity of their heart, soul and mind. For some, this may literally mean to 'shout for joy to the Lord, all the earth, burst into jubilant song with music; make music to the Lord with the harp, with the harp and the sound of singing, with trumpets and the blast of the ram's horn – shout for joy before the Lord, the King' (Ps 98:4–6). For other it might literally mean to 'be still and know that I am God; I will be exalted among the nations, I will be exalted in the earth' (Ps 46:10).

In a multiethnic church, encourage everyone to worship God however their heart chooses to express itself. Make sure to keep enough formality to the service and its start times to ensure there is order and some level of cohesiveness. Remember that Paul admonished the Corinthians for their lack of order when observing the Lord's Supper (1 Corinthians 12). We must treasure the communal worship time that we have once a week, humbly remembering that many people in persecuted communities aren't so lucky. At the same time, avoid being bogged down by the same old repetitive songs. And as Mark DeYmaz stresses, leaders mustn't 'allow past experiences, personal preferences, or personalities, or those things with which we are most comfortable with, or that we can more easily control, dictate what we do and how we do it. For if we acquiesce, we will surely build a church filled with other just like us'.[182]

Lastly know that the giftings and capacity of the leaders are finite and much of the style your church will embrace is dependent on those leading worship. It is all well and good for people to want a more choir appeal or to integrate some more multicultural instruments into the service, but they must be willing to make it happen. It is one thing to take many suggestions, but people need to step up and make it happen. All you can do is build a culture whereby members feel responsible for making the most out of the church experience rather than expecting everybody else to make things happen.

To finish, the chief principle your church should uphold in communal worship can be found in Paul's letter to the Philippians. Consider it a privilege to be able to worship together with brothers and sisters who are different from you.

> Do nothing out of selfish ambition or vain conceit. Rather, in humility value others above yourselves, not looking to your own interests but each of you to the interests of the others (Phil 2:3–4).

APPENDIX 6
BACK TO ANTIOCH

The Scriptures give us a precedent for diverse leadership. To discover this, let's return to our study of Antioch: 'In the church at Antioch there were prophets and teachers: Barnabas, Simeon called Niger, Lucius of Cyrene, Manaen (who had been brought up with Herod the tetrarch) and Saul' (Acts 13:1). Here we see Antioch leading the way with not only a diverse congregation but a diverse leadership team as well.

We are told of five leaders. I've already drawn attention to Paul's diversity as a Jewish rabbi and Roman citizen from Tarsus (modern day Turkey) schooled in Greek philosophy. There was also Barnabas, a Levite from the Mediterranean Island of Cyprus. Alongside these two are three interesting figures who up until this point were unknown in the story of Acts: Simeon called Niger, who was probably from somewhere in Africa

(*Niger* was a Latinism meaning 'black');[183] Lucius from Cyrene in North Africa (near modern day Libya); and Manaen, who (as we can deduce by the reference to Herod) was from somewhere in Palestine, potentially Judea, Galilee or maybe even Samaria. So, in this one church we have one leader from Asia Minor, one from the Mediterranean, one from the Middle East and two from Africa. Three different continents!

Mark DeYmaz rightly observes, 'It is interesting that Luke lists these men not only by name but also by ethnicity'.[184] There is no question that Luke has a purpose in listing these men's ethnicity. As David Peterson notes, 'What is most obvious is the ethnic diversity of the leadership of this church'.[185] Antioch was a remarkable church, and the diverse backgrounds of these five leaders were 'appropriate to the cosmopolitan context of Antioch'.[186]

Although there is a wider debate about whether the book of Acts is descriptive of the early church as opposed to being prescriptive for the contemporary church, what we *can* say is that Antioch's inclusion of a diverse leadership team has important implications for us today. The only way for a multiethnic church to flourish in the heterogeneous city of Antioch was for the appointment of diverse leadership. These leaders held the offices of prophets and teachers. In other words, they occupied profile positions within the life of the church. The brethren were united in Antioch because of it. Our churches must do the same today. From the pulpit down, people from diverse backgrounds need to be seen by your congregation in prominent positions.

At Parkside, it has been a real blessing as we've started to see the fruits of raising up leaders from all backgrounds. The closer that I get to retirement, the more I've prayed to God to raise up leaders, and today I can see the answers to those prayers beginning to blossom. In recent years, we've had as many as seven leaders attend Bible College for training in Christian ministry. We can never underestimate the supernatural intervention of God as we seek to raise up diverse leadership.

A TIP FOR MONOETHNIC CHURCHES – 'SET APART FOR ME'

> While they were worshipping the Lord and fasting, the Holy Spirit said, 'Set apart for me Barnabas and Saul for the work to which I have called them' (Acts 13:1b–2).

A common objection to diverse leadership may come from those in monoethnic churches who have trouble finding someone of a different ethnic background internally in order to appoint them to a position of leadership. The concern is a valid one and is not addressed easily. The only solution is to go external. This may not always be feasible, as financial constraints can be a hindrance to appointing new staff. More to the point, it is difficult to take someone from a completely different culture and plant them in a monoethnic community.

When I came to Parkside, the church took a tremendous risk in appointing me. They were an exclusively white congregation, whereas I was of Indian descent, and English was only my second language. But God's anointing was on us all.

One suggested starting point for your church is to consider the possibility of church partnerships as a means for creating diversity in leadership. It may be that there is a church nearby seeking to achieve the same multiethnic direction as you but coming from a different cultural background. Partnering with other churches can be a foreign concept, but what better way could there be for two churches, who are seeking to become more multiethnic but struggling, to create a plurality of leadership than through this 'set apart for me' type strategy. Now what I mean by this is temporarily exposing leaders in your church to a different cultural setting. Almost like a leadership swap type thing. Not a swap in the sense that you handover all the leadership, but rather like a student foreign exchange situation. Set them apart to do work experience with people in a different ethnic background. Such a swap might just be a catalyst for your church in becoming accustomed to different leadership styles.

What I put forward may not seem attractive, but there is some scriptural backing for this. As seen in Acts 13:1–2, the church at Antioch was required by God to set apart Paul and Barnabas for the work of mission. Now if we are one body, as the Scriptures make clear (Romans 12:4, 1 Corinthians 12:12), what's wrong in setting leaders apart so that they may continue the work of strengthening other churches? It is a sacrifice and requires a global vision far beyond the local church environment. It must have been a sacrifice for Antioch to lose two well-established leaders, but it was God's calling and just read the rest of Acts to see what eventuated from this sacrifice. Another example is when the Apostle Paul reached out to the local churches in Rome, Corinth and Galatia when the church in Jerusalem was in financial need (Rom 15:22–32; Cor 16:1–4; 2 Cor 8:1—9:15). He basically said to these churches, 'You have resources that are desperately needed elsewhere in the body'. A more global perspective entails that we are alert to the possibility of some leaders being set apart for the purposes of going to other churches where there is a dearth of leadership.

APPENDIX 7
SEND THE OTHERS TO KFC

> That night all the members of the community raised their voices and wept aloud. All the Israelites grumbled against Moses and Aaron, and the whole assembly said to them, 'If only we had died in Egypt! Or in this wilderness! Why is the Lord bringing us to this land only to let us fall by the sword? Our wives and children will be taken as plunder. Wouldn't it be better for us to go back to Egypt?' And they said to each other, 'We should choose a leader and go back to Egypt' (Num 14:1–4).

You are probably wondering what happens when key leaders in a church are resistant to changes towards multiethnic worship. This is a common issue, especially when a person has become used to doing something or has been leading a ministry for a long time and is resistant to change. If you are to transform a monoethnic church into and multiethnic one, there will be some major changes, which ministry leaders may be reluctant to embrace. You must be aware that resistance doesn't only come from the average church member. Church members tend to be easier to deal with; if they think the grass is greener on the other side, they eventually leave to check out that greener grass. If such people leave to go elsewhere, it can be a blessing, because they take their negative voices with them. But when those grumbling voices are your leaders, or very influential members of the congregation who whisper into the ears of others, it can be much harder. As Moses encountered, there are always grumbling voices saying, 'Let's go back to Egypt'. It is a hard thing when these voices get to your leaders and they end up getting frustrated and leaving (especially if they leave ministry altogether). Worse still, some people in your congregation may continuously grumble in an attempt to outlast your patience. Unfortunately for these people, when they grumble against you they are grumbling against God's appointed leader and they will answer to him. Nonetheless, churches can get into this cycle and end up building a 'revolving door' culture, with leader after leader after leader. Hopefully, if you've done your best to educate leaders on the biblical mandate behind your changes and you've given adequate time for incremental changes and input from others, you should have less and less of this.

Division, when prevalent in a church, is poisonous, especially when it is among the leadership. That's what the enemy wants to achieve. He wants to inject a lethal dose of poison into the church, and the most effective way for him to do this is to target the leadership. Be prepared for the spiritual battle, and make sure you are willing to make changes to leadership if necessary.

I have experienced this toxin in the past. In the early days at Parkside, I faced a tremendous amount of opposition. The worst of this came from those in leadership. At one point, one among my own deacons was plotting against me. They wanted me gone. Even once we were well on our way with the vision, I still experienced disunity at times. We must remember that any leader who opposes God's universal mission for a multiethnic church should not be in a position of leadership. If they are stubbornly unwilling to be a part of that vision, then you must cut them loose – even if it is only for some time.

There's a great Bible story that illustrates this need to cut your leadership loose. John 4 records one of the most radical things Christ did. The famous story is of Jesus in dialogue with a Samaritan woman. The story starts with Jesus deciding to go through Samaria. While his disciples are out getting lunch, he begins a conversation with a Samarian lady. Now Jesus does several countercultural things in this story. First, he chooses to go through Samaria. As we've already seen, the Jewish people absolutely despised the Samaritans. At the time of Jesus, the relationship was so severe that a Jew would not even travel through a Samarian village; instead, they would take a longer route to go all the way around just to avoid them. Simply by being in a Samarian village to begin with, Jesus is skating on thin ice. Second, Jesus as a Jewish man chooses to start a conversation with this Samaritan woman, which was a social taboo. Third, he asks her to get him a drink. All guys know that if you do that at a bar, you end up wearing her drink! 'The Samaritan woman said to him, "You are a Jew and I am a Samaritan woman. How can you ask me for a drink?" (For Jews do not associate with Samaritans)' (John 4:9).

Nevertheless, it is interesting that Jesus sends his disciple out to get lunch before initiating this conversation. Jesus would have known the remarkable outcome of this interaction. He was able to reveal to that lady the brokenness in her life and in turn reveal who he was, and with that she became the first evangelist in the New Testament. She went back and brought the entire village to hear Jesus. This surely would have been a remarkable learning opportunity for the disciples to have witnessed, especially if he wanted them to know how to evangelise cross-culturally. So why does he send them to get lunch? Because he knew if they were there, this may never have happened. Think about it. The first thing the disciples do when they get back is show that they're indignant. They can't believe that Jesus is breaking all cultural customs. They are critical, but they're just not brave enough to vocalise what they're really thinking: 'Just then his disciples returned and were surprised to find him talking with a woman. But no one asked, "What do you want?" or "Why are you talking with her?"' (John 4:27).

Many leaders can be like this. Yet Jesus remained gospel-centred in his approach. Jesus knew that his church must be multiethnic. He knew that in order for this to occur, he needed to be the one to start breaking down ethnic and cultural barriers. And, while he did that, he opted to send his disciples off to KFC, so to speak. That way, they wouldn't get in the way.

Always remember Jesus' words to his disciples, when the tough times came and people left. Jesus asked, 'You do not want to leave too, do you? (John 6:67). We know that by the time of the cross, the disciples, in their fear, *did* want to leave. But that wasn't going to stop Jesus; he was prepared to give people an out clause. He was prepared to tell them to go. And he was also prepared to welcome them back as leaders, even after they left.

A leader truly committed to the vision of a multiethnic church must be prepared, as Jesus was, to do both: to show people the door and the way back to Egypt, if that's where they want to go, but also to welcome them back and reinstate them as leaders if they get on board with the vision. The greatest opposers can become the greatest supporters. Remember, even individuals like Paul, Peter, Thomas and James at one point or another expressed doubt or opposition towards Jesus' ministry.

APPENDIX 8
THE ROLE OF WOMEN

At our multiethnic conference, held in Sydney in 2012, we were engaging in a Q&A with the speakers when the topic of women in ministry came up. If you're breaking down the ethnic barrier, it is not a surprise that questions arise about whether you are committed to doing the same with the gender barrier.

Unfortunately, a detailed examination of this subject is well beyond the parameters of this book. Neither is there scope to give a detailed theological commentary on contentious passages like 1 Corinthians 14:34 or 1 Timothy 2:12 or to outline in any length the competing positions of egalitarianism (all ministry roles are open to any gender) and complementarianism (some ministry roles can and should be distinguished by gender). However, because of the importance of this topic, I thought it only appropriate to offer a few points with respect to how this plays out in a multiethnic church.

In multiethnic churches – like all other churches – the role of women is vital. We see woman playing a very important role in the New Testament: Priscilla, Chloe, Lydia, Apphia, Nympha, Tryphena and Tryphosa (see John 4:1–44, Luke 8:2–3, Acts: 1:14, 21:9, 16:13–15, 17:4, 12, 34, 18:3, Rom 16:1–16), to name a few. At Parkside, we recognise the importance of having women on the pastoral staff team and occupying positions of senior leadership across all ministries and the deaconate.

However, in a multiethnic church the question becomes quite grey. We deal with a conundrum: on the one hand striving to break down both ethnic and gender barriers, while on the other hand trying to avoid causing others to stumble. Whether one likes it or not, the reality is that in some cultures, particularly Middle Eastern cultures, the role of women in religious leadership is not practised. For a new person from these cultural backgrounds, seeing women preaching and teaching is something unfamiliar and potentially very uncomfortable. This is not always the case; I have seen very traditional monoethnic churches that are surprisingly open and comfortable with women preaching. In contrast, for a Westerner it would be considered equally confrontational not to have women involved equally in the participation of the church. It would be considered sexist and wrong.

Add to this the fact that each church denomination (or non-denomination) has its own beliefs and practices around the subject of female ordination, and it gets complicated. In the Baptist circles within which we operate, female ordination is open to both men and women. However (there's always a but), because church autonomy is a fundamental belief in the Baptist denomination, no association can mandate a set of theological convictions for individual churches. Hence, you get some Baptist churches that encourage and support women in ordained roles, and others that don't practise formal female ordination. It was due to this very issue that the Baptist association we are affiliated with, Baptist Churches of NSW and ACT, opted years ago to have a separate system for accrediting new ministers so as not to diminish the local church's autonomy. Under this system, the wider association will accredit new ministers, but it is the responsibility of the local church to set them apart for service and ordain them. This means that, while the association will accredit men and woman equally for ministry, no individual church is required to ordain female ministers should it conflict with their theological leanings.

Therefore, true to the autonomous nature of our church, we do not have the solution, nor will we endeavour to reconcile the issue for your church.

We should recognise that there is common ground held by both camps on a few points. First, both recognise that women certainly must play a pivotal role in the life and leadership of the church. The New Testament does not shy away from the fact that women played a crucial role in early church: they were first witnesses to the resurrection of Jesus (Matt 28:1; Mark 16:1;

Luke 24:1; John 20:1), were involved in church planting and meetings (Acts 16:14–15; 1 Cor 1:11) and held positions of leadership (Rom 16:3–5; Acts 18:24–28; Phil 4:2–3).[187] Second, both camps recognise that there are some gender-related ministries (for example, women's and men's groups and one-on-one counselling or mentoring) where wisdom requires gender-specific appointments.

The question remains: how do you honour your theological convictions on the subject without causing unnecessary stumbling blocks, all while trying to remain culturally fair-minded? Some people passionately consider female ordination a matter of equality; others passionately believe that endorsing it is not faithful to Scripture. In the wider Christian movement, we must recognise that we don't have a unified solution to this. It is up to each individual and church to make up their own mind based on theological reflection and be prepared to educate those people and cultural groups within your church who don't share that same conviction or practice. In a sense, this is the same approach we should take with any hot topic ethical issue. Where the Scriptures are clear, we mustn't compromise or reinterpret. (This is the mistake many are making in this generation when it comes to controversial issues like same-sex marriage. They are taking clear scriptural evidence and trying to reinterpret it.)

Now in saying that, I understand there will be some on both sides who feel that the other camp is the one reinterpreting what they feel to be clear scriptural guidelines. At the very least, we must come to common ground and note that on the subject of women preaching and teaching, there is not widespread agreement among theologians. Therefore, it is important for us to show love, respect and grace to each other whether we find agreement or not. It is incumbent on all within the body of Christ to show humility when it comes to subjects like this. I do not believe Jesus would want us behaving in a pharisaical way over such matters. We mustn't confuse the inerrancy of Scripture with our own interpretations of Scripture. God's word is inerrant; our interpretations are not.

If you have exegeted both the Scriptures and your cultural setting and feel clear that it would be too much of a stumbling block to have women doing things like preaching and teaching, then removing this stumbling block is what you must do. As a corollary to this, however, I enjoin that sometimes we must be culturally inappropriate to be Christ-appropriate. If certain cultural groups hold values contra to biblical Christianity, they must be stood against intentionally. Consequently, those cultures that are hyper-patriarchal need a dose of biblical Christianity. In the past I've worked with a mission organisation who did not ordain female pastors. As someone serving in the field, I actually had to bring to their attention that, in practice, some women were basically carrying out all the functions of a minister without being recognised. They were ministering among native people and were fulfilling the responsibilities of teaching, preaching, disciplining and so on because there was no one else available. These faithful women were the only ones who had the biblical training and needed to be the ones to lead the male converts.

Hyper-patriarchal cultures need to recognise that, just as our ethnicity does not determine our right standing before God, neither does our gender; God wishes all the men and women he saves to use their spiritual gifts to pronounce that message of salvation to the world. How and in what capacity God wishes them to serve in the body is up to him to determine.

Alternatively, if having exegeted the Scriptures you believe that your expression of church can accommodate for women and men to engage equally in church vocation, and the majority of those in the church espouse the same beliefs, then go forward with that. The caution here is to be wary that not all cultures are as open to women engaging in public meetings as you may be. This issue was the same in the days of the early church. Be prepared to work even harder to win those types of people and remember that part of our gospel responsibility is to be culturally appropriate and forgo our rights if need be. This follows the proverbial logic of Paul: 'To the weak I became weak, to win the weak. I have become all things to all people so that by all possible means I might save some' (1 Cor 9:22).

I understand that what I've outlined here may not be entirely satisfactory, especially for those who hold firm on their position and would have preferred that I espoused a clear view that agreed with their position. Unfortunately, this is just one of those issues that we must leave unanswered. Regrettably, people do leave churches over this issue. Our main concern here, however, is to recognise that this issue is one that multiethnic churches must work hard to make sure they get it right. The solution is not straightforward.

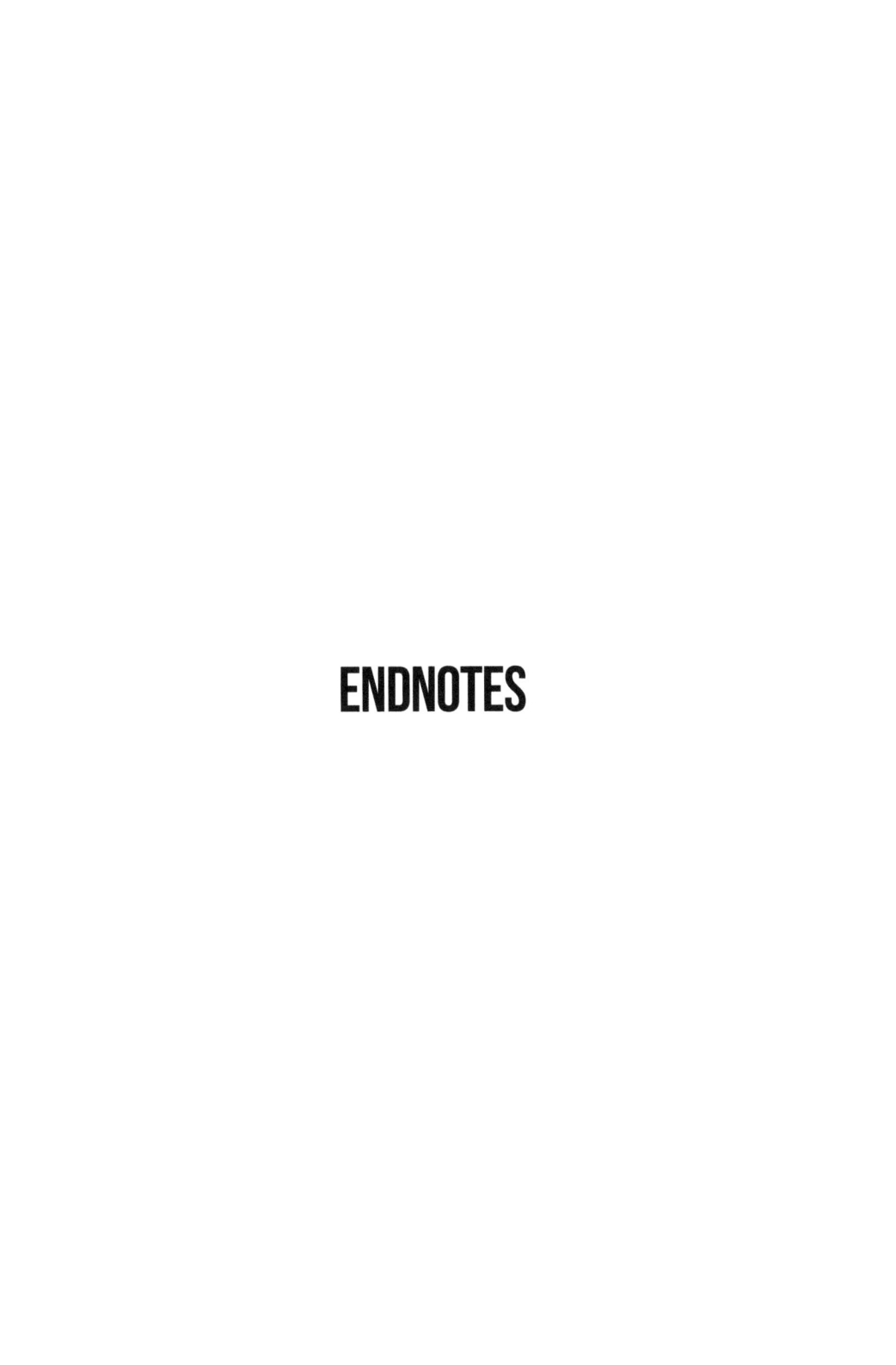

ENDNOTES

ENDNOTES

Introduction

1   This quote has traditionally been ascribed to Martin Luther King. See David Van Biema, 'Can Megachurches Bridge the Racial Divide?' *Time Magazine* 175, no. 1 (Jan 2010), http://content.time.com/time/magazine/article/0,9171,1950943,00.html.

2   Curtiss Paul Deyoung, *United by Faith: The Multiracial Congregation as an Answer to the Problems of Race*, (New York: Oxford University Press, 2003), 2.

3   Donald Sommerville, *The Complete Illustrated History of World War Two: An Authoritative Account of the Deadliest Conflict in Human History with Analysis of Decisive Encounters and Landmark Engagements* (Leicester: Lorenz Books, 2008), 5.

4   There are many other examples where ethnic segregation (alongside things like religion and politics) has resulted in conflicts: the Partition of India in 1947, based on religious demographics and the subsequent split of Pakistan and Bangladesh; the Civil War in China (1927–1950); the Civil Wars in Korea (25 June 1950 – 27 July 1953); the series of Indochinese Wars (1946–1979); the Sri Lankan Civil War (1982–2009). The Middle East has also been synonymous with warfare, political revolts, border disputes and the like. In most recent years the major occurrences include: The Six Day War (1967), The Gulf War (1990–1991), Iraq War (2003–2011), War in Afghanistan (2001–present), and even the present crisis which has sprung up since the Arab Springs of 2011.

5   Take, for instance, the Vatican's policy of neutrality in World War II. See Owen Chadwick, *Britain and the Vatican During the Second World War* (Cambridge, UK: Cambridge University Press, 1986), 115, 127, 131, 223, 224. By no means do I seek to diminish the extensive humanitarian efforts made by some figures in the Catholic Church. For instance, Hugh O'Flaherty, an Irish priest, has been credited with helping to save 6,500 Jewish and Allied escapees. See article by Majella O'Sullivan, *Vatican's 'Scarlet Pimpernel' Honoured, Irish Independent*, (12/11/2012), http://www.independent.ie/irish-news/vaticans-scarlet-pimpernel-honoured-28895222.html. I also acknowledge the likes of Maximilian Kolbe, who was arrested for his efforts to hide Polish refugees including over 2,000 Jewish refugees. He made an incredible sacrifice, while in Auschwitz he died in place of a fellow prisoner. However, although there were a few Protestants like Dietrich Bonhoeffer who actively stood against Nazism, most Lutheran churches saluted Hitler. For a helpful resource on the subject, I recommend Robert P. Eriksen and Susannah Heschel, eds., *Betrayal: German Churches and the Holocaust* (Minneapolis: Augsburg Fortress Publishers, 1999).

6   The exact timing of this migration is still widely debated. For further analysis see, 'When did Australia's earliest inhabitants arrive?' University of Wollongong, 2004, viewed 4 September 2014, <http://media.uow.edu.au/news/2004/0917a/index.html>.

7   Mollie Gillen, *The Founders of Australia: A Biographical Dictionary of the First Fleet* (Sydney: Library of Australian History, 1989), 445.

8   Figures were obtained from the Australian Government, Department of Immigration and Citizenship, *Fact Sheet 2 – Key Facts about Immigration*, http://www.immi.gov.au/media/fact-sheets/02key.htm?. The number would have changed by the time you read this.

9   Australian Government, Department of Immigration and Citizenship, *Fact Sheet 4 – More than 65 Years of Post-war Migration*, http://www.immi.gov.au/media/fact-sheets/04fifty.htm.

10 Gemma Jones, 'Asylum emergency off Christmas Island pushes number of boat arrivals under Labor to 50,000', news.com.au, News Limited, August 6, 2013, http://www.news.com.au/national-news/federal-election/asylum-emergency-off-christmas-island-pushes-number-of-boat-arrivals-under-labor-to-50000/story-fnho52ip-1226692388773. Please note that by 'without permit', I mean that upon arrival they were not on any government or international body waiting list.

11 Mark DeYmaz, *Building a Healthy Multiethnic Church: Mandate, Commitments and Practices of a Diverse Congregation* (San Francisco: John Wiley & Son, 2007), xxx.

12 Rodney Woo, *The Color of the Church: A Biblical and Practical Paradigm for Multiracial Churches* (Nashville: B&H Publishing Group, 2009), 14.

ENDNOTES

13 Deyoung et al., *United by Faith*, 2.

14 Ibid.

15 Woo, *Color*, 13.

Chapter 1

16 'Kerala Religion Census 2011', *Census 2011*, http://www.census2011.co.in/data/religion/state/32-kerala.html.

17 Hinduism constitutes about 80 per cent, with Islam between 14–15 per cent. See 'Religion', *Office of the Registrar General and Census Commissioner, India* http://censusindia.gov.in/Census_And_You/religion.aspx.

18 T. K. Joseph, *Six St. Thomases Of South India*, (University of California, 1955), 27.

19 See Augustine Kanjamala, *The Future of Christian Mission in India: Toward a New Paradigm for the Third Millennium* Missional Church, Public Theology, World Christianity 4 (Pickwick Publications, 2014), 171–72.

20 Maya George, *Faith and Philosophy of Christianity* (Delhi: Kalpaz Publications, 2009), 280.

21 In the 2011 census it was around the 60 per cent mark. See *Reflecting a Nation: Stories from the 2011 Census, 2012–2013*, Australian Bureau of Statistics, http://www.abs.gov.au/ausstats/abs@.nsf/Latestproducts/2071.0Main%20Features902012%E2%80%932013. At the time of writing, the 2016 census data has not been made available, but all the available data suggest its around 52 per cent. Based on a 2017 'Faith and Belief' survey done by McCrindle Research, only around 45 per cent identify as practicing Christians. The categories were widened from the 2016 national census to include 'spiritual but not religious'. This category made up 14 per cent. See Mark McCrindle, *Faith and Belief in Australia: A National Study on Religion, Spirituality and Worldview Trends* (NSW: A McCrindle Publication, 2017), 7–8.

22 Ibid. McCrindle research highlights that of the 45 per cent who identify with Christianity, only 15per cent attend church regularly and about 22 per cent less than annually or not at all.

23 For more detailed commentary on the state of play in Australia, I recommend Tom Frame, *Losing My Religion: Unbelief in Australia*, (Sydney: UNSW Press Book, 2009).

Chapter 2

24 Charles Edward van Engen, *God's Missionary People: Rethinking the Purpose of the Local Church* (Grand Rapids, MI: Baker Book House, 1991), 126.

25 I like the way Brandon Cox, former Pastor at Saddleback, describes it in 'Why I Hope the Multiethnic Ministry Conversation is Short-Lived', http://pastors.com/why-i-hope-the-multiethnic-ministry-conversation-is-short-lived/: 'My prayer is that planting and leading churches that are ethnically representative of the diversity in their surrounding communities will become so normal and commonplace that we don't have to talk about a strategy for getting it done anymore'.

26 Josephus, *Antiquities* xvii 9.5.

27 All of our fact and figures have been obtained directly from the UNHCR website as at August 2017. Please note, these are changing all the time. See Figures at a Glance: Statistical Year Book, *UNHCR: The UN Refugee Agency*, http://www.unhcr.org/en-au/figures-at-a-glance.html.

28 In the LXX, the term was also used to designate the public gathering of Israel in Deuteronomy 4:10. For further examination of the term see Ben Witherington, *Conflict and Community in Corinth: A Socio-Rhetorical Commentary on 1 and 2 Corinthians* (Grand Rapids, MI: Eerdmans, 1995), 79–80; Gordon D. Fee, *The First Epistle to the Corinthians* NICNT (Grand Rapids, MI: Eerdmans, 1987), 31–32.

29 Tom Steers, 'Needed: More Monocultural Ministries: Why Christians shouldn't try to fit every ethnic group into the same ministry mold', *Christianity Today* July 2010, http://www.christianitytoday.com/ct/2010/julyweb-only/37-31.0.html.

30 Josephus, *Antiquities* 18.63–64. See John Dickson, *The Christ Files* (Grand Rapids, MI: Zondervan, 2005), 43–44.

31 Steers, 'Needed: More Monocultural Ministries'.

32 DeYmaz, *Building*, 27.

Chapter 3

33 Barry Webb, *The Message of Isaiah*, BST (Leister: IVP, 1996), 30–31.

34 Allan Harman, *Isaiah, A Covenant to Be Kept for the Sake of the Church* (Scotland: Christian Focus Publications, 2005), 379.

35 For a simple description of the history of the Jewish temple see B. Chilton, P.W. Comfort and M. O. Wise, 'Temple Jewish' in *Dictionary of the New Testament Background*, edited by Craig A. Evans and Stanley E. Porter (Downers Grove: IVP, 2000), 1167–8.

ENDNOTES

36 Ibid., 1168.

37 Alec Garrard, *The Splendor of the Temple*, (Grand Rapids: Kregel Publications, 2000), 44.

38 Joachim Jeremias, *Jerusalem in the Time of Jesus: An Investigation into Economic and Social Conditions During the New Testament Period* (Philadelphia: Fortress, 1969), 48–49; John D. Davis, *A Dictionary of the Bible* (Philadelphia: Westminster, 1923), 765.

39 E. P. Sanders, *The Historical Figure of Jesus* (England: Penguin Books, 1993), 249. Others have put the estimates much higher. For our discussions, it doesn't matter.

40 Christopher Wright has been the leading voice on mission as an important theme in the Old Testament. According to Wright, God's mission to redeem all of humanity begins with a selected nation. The theme of mission is the key to unlocking the Bible's overarching narrative. See *The Mission of God: Unlocking the Bible's Grand Narrative* (Downers Grove: IVP Academic, 2006).

41 Junius P. Rodriguez, *The Historical Encyclopedia of World Slavery*, Volume 1 (Santa Barbara, CA: ABC-CLIO, 1997), 243.

Chapter 4

42 We should not make the mistake of believing that the Holy Spirit only emerges at Pentecost. Already in his Gospel, Luke emphasises and builds a theology around the Holy Spirit as an important part of salvation history. The mission of God is a Trinitarian one. See Luke 1:15, 35; 3:16; 4:1, 14, 18; 24:49. For further thoughts, see Darrell L. Block, *A Theology of Luke-Acts: God's Promised Program, Realised for All Nations* (Grand Rapids, Michigan: Zondervan, 2012), 211–26.

43 See comments on structure by David G. Peterson, *The Acts of the Apostles*, Pillar NTC (Nottingham: Apollos, 2009), 32–36, 112–13.

44 Chrysostom, *Pan. Ign.* 4; Pliny *Nat. Hist.* 6.122. Population figures differ because it is not clear how slaves functioned in these counts. See L. M. McDonald, 'Antioch (Syria)', in *Dictionary of the New Testament Background*, Craig A. Evans and Stanley E. Porter (Downers Grove Illinios, IVP, 2000), 34.

45 Strabo *Geog.* 16.25. Ajith Fernando, *Act, The NIV Application Commentary* (Grand Rapids, Michigan: Zondervan, 1998); J McRay, 'Antioch on the Orontes', in *Dictionary of Paul and His Letters*, edited by G.F. Hawthorne, R. P. Martin and D.G. Reid (Downers Grove, Illinois: IVP, 1993), 23.

46 The city was connected to spice trade routes, the Silk Road and the trade highway known as the Persian Royal Road. McDonald, 'Antioch (Syria)', 34.

47 Ibid. 34.

48   Ibid. 34–35. See Josephus, *Jewish Wars* 7.3.3§43.

49   McRay, 'Antioch', 23.

50   Ibid. 23 'A huge wealthy and cosmopolitan city where barriers for religion, race and nationality were easily crossed – and where toleration may have been a matter of civic pride .....'

51   Josephus JW 7.3.3§45.

52   McRay, 'Antioch', 23–24.

53   DeYmaz, *Building*, 3–11.

54   Ibid., 9–10.

55   Key proponents have included David Bosch, Leslie Newbigin, Alan Hirsch, Miroslav Volf, Tim Keller and Michael Frost. The Latin term has a history at least as far back as Augustine. During the 1930s, Karl Hartenstein was a modern prominent who coined the term to suggest the church's mission was to participate in God's plan to establish the lordship of Christ. Tormod Engelsviken, 'Missio Dei: The Understanding and Misunderstanding of a Theological Concept in European Churches and Missiology', *International Review of Mission* 92, no. 4 (2003): 482. Certainly, by the 1950s a clearer placement of mission within the doctrine of the Triune God was being formulated. See Richard Niebuhr, 'An Attempt at a Theological Analysis of Missionary Motivation', *Occasional Bulletin of Missionary Research* 14, no. 1 (1963): 1–6.

56   Scholars have attributed Karl Barth as identifying mission not as a church program but as an activity of God himself. Paul Winch, 'Exploring Theological Bearing', *Servantship: Sixteen Servants in the Four Movements of Radical Servantship*, edited by G. Hill (Eugene, OR: Wipf and Stock, 2013), 103.

57   David Bosch, *Transforming Mission: Paradigm Shifts in Theology of Mission* (Maryknoll, NY: Orbis, 1991), 390: 'Mission is not primarily an activity of the church, but an attribute of God. Mission is thereby seen as a movement from God to the world; the church is viewed as an instrument for that mission'.

58   Graeme Anderson, 'Forming a Missional and Trinitarian Church', in Hill, *Servantship*, 68.

59   Winch, 'Exploring Theological Bearing', 103. Jurgen Moltmann articulated it by stating, 'It is not the church that has a mission of salvation to fulfil in the world; it is the mission of the Son and the Spirit through the Father that includes the church'. See *The Church in the Power of the Spirit: A Contribution to Messianic Ecclesiology* (London: SCM Press, 1977), 64. See also Darrell L. Guder, 'Missional Theology for a Missionary Church', *Journal for Preachers* 22 no. 1 (1998): 5; Anderson, 'Forming', 68–69; Michael Frost, *The Big Ideas: the Great Themes of Evangelism* (Macquarie Park, NSW: Morling Press, 2011), 17–19; Rod MacIlvaine, 'What is the Missional Church Movement?', *Bibliotheca sacra* 167 no.

ENDNOTES

665 (2010): 96.

60   Eddie Gibbs, *Church Next: Quantum Changes in How We Do Ministry* (Downers Grove, IL: IVP, 2000), 56.

61   John Stott, *The Message of Acts*, BST (Nottingham: IVP, 1990), 200–201.

62   Ibid., 200.

63   McRay, 'Antioch', 24.

64   Stott, *Acts,* 205.

65   F. Scott Spencer, *Acts* (Sheffield, Sheffield Academic Press, 1997), 121.

66   According to Stowers, it can be linked to the common Hellenistic greeting 'chairein'. Stanley K. Stowers, *Letter Writing in Greco-Roman Antiquity* (Philadelphia: Westminster, 1986), 21.

67   Colin G. Kruse, *Paul's Letter to the Romans* PNTC (Grand Rapids, MI/Nottingham, England: Eerdmans/Apollos, 2012), 55–56; Joseph Fitzmyer, *Romans* (New York: Doubleday, 1993), 228.

68   Craig S. Keener, *Revelation* NIVAC (Grand Rapids, MI: Zondervan, 2000), 68–69.

Chapter 5

69   The word Apocalypse (Revelation 1:1), which contemporary Bibles translate to 'revelation', comes from the Greek *apokalypsis* meaning 'unveiling'. The book itself combines several genres, including a letter to seven churches (1:4) containing early Christian prophecy, but the major genre is apocalyptic literature. Such literature was a common style of writing in the first and second centuries. Historians have found a number of other documents sharing the genre. Understanding the genre of Revelation as apocalyptic literature is essential to interpreting the meaning of the text. For further reading see David A. De Silva, *An Introduction to the New Testament: Contexts, Methods and Ministry Formation* (Downers Grove Ill: IVP/Apollos, 2004), 886–8.

70   Eschatology is simply a reference to the study of the end times.

71   Grant R. Osborn, *Revelation* ECNT (Grand Rapids MI: Baker Academic, 2002), 318.

72   Richard Bauckham, *The Climax of Prophecy: Studies on the Book of Revelation* (Edinburgh: T & T Clark, 1993), 225.

73   G. K Beale, *The Book of Revelation New International Greek Testament Commentary* (Grand Rapids: Eerdmans, 1999), 426.

74   Osborn, *Revelation*, 319.

75   Keener, *Revelation*, 246–7.

76   Philippians 2:6–11 has been regarded by the majority of scholars and theologians as a pre-Pauline, early church hymn. See Ben Witherington, *Paul's Letter to the Philippians: A Socio-Rhetorical Commentary* (USA: Eerdmans, 2011), 132; Gordon D. Fee, *Paul's Letter to the Philippians*, NICNT (Grand Rapids, MI: Eerdmans, 1995), 40; G. W. Hansen, *The Letter to the Philippians*, Pillar (Grand Rapids, MI: Eerdmans, 2009), 122–3. Although theologians have been fascinated by its widely debated theological references to the pre-existent nature of Christ, one should not overlook the Paul's central rhetorical purpose: an exhortation to unity. D.F. Watson, 'A Rhetorical Analysis of Philippians and Its Implications for the Unity Question', *Novum Testamentum* 30 (1988): 59–60.

Chapter 6

77   Nelson R. Mandela, *Long Walk to Freedom: The Autobiography of Nelson Mandela* (New York: Back Bay Books, 1995), 622.

78   James Jupp and John Nieuwenhuysen, *Social Cohesion in Australia* (Cambridge, New York: Cambridge University Press, 2007), 66.

79   Jock Collins, 'Sydney's Cronulla Riots: The Context and Implications', in *Lines in the Sand: the Cronulla Riots, Multiculturalism and National Belonging*, edited by G. Noble (Sydney: Institute of Criminology Press, 2009), 27.

80   Kate Warner, 'Gang Rape in Sydney: Crime, the Media, Politics, Race and Sentencing', *Australian and New Zealand Journal of Criminology* 37 no. 3, December 2004: 344–61.

81   The referenced article describes several cases of Middle Eastern individuals feeling greater discrimination since Cronulla. Brigid Delaney and Cynthia Banham, 'Muslims Feel the Hands of Racism Tighten Around Them', *Sydney Morning Herald* June 17, 2004, http://www.smh.com.au/articles/2004/06/16/1087244979369.html.

82   Australians have been the victims of acts of terrorism. Australians died in 9/11 and in the Bali Bombings, though these were not on home soil. Australia did experience an act of terrorism on home soil during the events of December 15–16, 2014, in what has become known as the Sydney Siege.

83   There are many detailed resources on the subject of the treatment of Indigenous Australians. For a couple of brief and easy introductions, I recommend some of the material found on the website of the Australian Institute of Aboriginal and Torres Strait Islander Studies: https://aiatsis.gov.au/. For access to the various Commonwealth government reports on some of the oppression, including the *Bringing them Home* report, see *Apology to Australia's Indigenous Peoples*, Australian Institute of Aboriginal and Torres Strait Islander Studies website,

ENDNOTES

       https://aiatsis.gov.au/explore/articles/apology-australias-indigenous-peoples.

84   John Stott, *Issues Facing Christians Today* (UK: Marshall, Morgan & Scott, 1984).

85   Ibid., 194–211.

86   Ibid., 209.

87   Cultural Diversity in Australia, Reflecting A Nation: Stories from the 2011 Census, Australian Bureau of Statistics, June 21, 2012, http://www.abs.gov.au/ausstats/abs@.nsf/Lookup/2071.0main+features902012-2013. These statistics are based on the most up-to-date data available. Australia held a national census in 2011 and in 2016. At the point of writing, not all of the data from the 2016 census has been made available. Where I can get the most current statistics, I have included them.

88   Ibid.

89   Joshua Maule, 'Multi-plication: Why Culturally Diverse Churches are the Future', *Eternity* 28, (2012): 5.

90   2011 Census data shows more than 300 ancestries reported in Australia, Media Release June 21, 2012, ABS, http://www.abs.gov.au/websitedbs/censushome.nsf/home/CO-62?opendocument&navpos=620.

91   The exact locations and historical time periods are still a subject of varying academic conjecture depending on which source you read. See Barbara A. West, *A Brief History of Australia* (USA: Facts on File, 2010), 13–17; Australian Government, *About Australia: Our Country*, http://australia.gov.au/about-australia/our-country.

92   James Jupp, *The Australian People: An Encyclopaedia of the Nation, Its People and Their Origin*s (UK: Cambridge University Press, repr 2001), 35.

93   Department of Immigration and Citizenship, *Immigration to Australia During the 20th Century – Historical Impacts on Immigration Intake, Population Size and Population Composition – A Timeline*, http://www.immi.gov.au/media/publications/statistics/federation/timeline1.pdf.

94   These countries were among the top ten sources of immigration. Source is based on a report commissioned by Department of Immigration and Multicultural Affairs, *Immigration: Federation to Century's End 1901–2000*, 2001, http://www.immi.gov.au/media/publications/statistics/federation/federation.pdf, 24.

95   Figures were obtained from the Australian Government, Department of Immigration and Citizenship, *Fact Sheet 2 – Key Facts about Immigration,* http://www.immi.gov.au/media/fact-sheets/02key.htm?.

96   Janet Philips and Joanne Simon-Davies, *Migration to Australia: A Quick Guide to the Statistics*, Parliament of Australia, last updated January 2017, http://www.aph.gov.au/About_Parliament/Parliamentary_Departments/Parliamentary_Library/pubs/rp/rp1617/Quick_Guides/MigrationStatistics.

97 For the full transcript see: 'Pauline Hanson's 1996 Maiden Speech to Parliament: Full Transcript', *Sydney Morning Herald*, September 2016, http://www.smh.com.au/federal-politics/political-news/pauline-hansons-1996-maiden-speech-to-parliament-full-transcript-20160914-grgjv3.html. I need to be a little cautious quoting Pauline Hanson. Hanson lost her seat in Federal parliament in the late 1990s, only to successfully recontest a position in the Senate in 2016. Since then she has nuanced her position, and the views she holds now may be different to those she held earlier. As an independent and not part of one of the major parties, she has in the past represented genuine concerns people have held.

98 Stott, *Issues Facing Christians*, 209.

Chapter 8

99 For a similar reflection see Bob R. Agee, 'Leadership, Vision and Strategic Planning', in *Christian Leadership Essentials: A Handbook for Managing Christian Organizations*, edited by David S. Dockery (Nashville: B&H Publishing Group, 2001), 46–49.

100 See Rick Warren, *The Purpose Driven Church: Growing Without Compromising Your Message and Mission* (Grand Rapids: Zondervan, 1995), 169–72.

101 Ibid., 155–7.

102 DeYmaz, *Building*, 56.

103 Ibid., 57.

104 Mark DeYmaz and Harry Li, *Ethnic Blends: Mixing Diversity into Your Local Church* (Grand Rapids, MI: Zondervan, 2010), 48.

105 The background reason for this had to do with the foreign policy employed by the Assyrian rulers. They believed that if different ethnic groups were mixed together, they would be less likely to rise up in rebellion. However, for those from the Southern Kingdom (which followed the Davidic kingly line), when the new Babylonian superpower conquered Jerusalem in 587 BC, the foreign policy was slightly different. The Babylonians sought to carry the captives off into exile and chose the best and brightest (those like Daniel, Shadrach, Meshach and Abednego) to be educated in the Babylonian traditions and then returned to their pocket communities as pro-Babylonian administrators.

106 For a deeper understanding of the relationship between the Jewish people and the Samaritans, see H.G.M. Williamson and C.A. Evans, 'Samaritans' in *Dictionary of the New Testament Background*, edited by Craig A. Evans and Stanley E. Porter (Downers Grove: IVP, 2000), 1056–60.

107 Michael Frost and Alan Hirsch, *The Shaping of Things to Come: Innovation and Mission for the 21st-Century Church*, revised edition (Grand Rapids: Baker Books, 2013), 67.

ENDNOTES

Chapter 9

108   Please note I've changed some of the names in retelling this story.

109   When the New Testament authors speak of the Greeks, they use the root word Hellén. When Paul refers to 'the Greeks' in his pronouncement and throughout his letters, he is not simply referring to those from native Greece. During Paul's time – as was also the case in later history – the term became synonymous with a much larger group of people who were Greek-speaking and who followed Greek culture and philosophy, regardless of ethnicity. The conquests of Alexander the Great left a lasting cultural impact, on the entire Mediterranean/Near East region in areas of language, philosophy, literature, art, athletics and entertainment. This was known as Hellenism. *Koine* Greek, meaning 'common' Greek, became the dominant spoken language. A modern equivalent would be the impact British and American cultures have had on forming 'Western culture'. Although many Jews would have been influenced by Hellenistic culture and spoken *Koine* Greek, they typically attempted to retain their cultural exclusivity.

110   Clinton Arnold, 'Ephesus', in *Dictionary of Paul and His Letters*, edited by Gerald F. Hawthorne and Ralph P. Martin (Downers Grove, Illinios: IVP, 1993), 249.

111   The Ephesians erected temples dedicated to Julius Caesar and Augustus and colossal statues to other members of the imperial household including Claudius, Nero and Domitian, which were placed in prominent civic areas. In Acts 19:23–41 the controversial preaching of Paul and his companions attracted the fury of the craftsmen industry, provoking a riot in the city.

112   For further discussion about the city see Arnold, 'Ephesus', 249–53; De Silva, *Introduction*, 714–16.

113   Josephus *Ant.* 13.3.2 §125.

114   Arnold, 'Ephesus', 251.

115   Although there is still dispute among scholars over the Pauline authorship, I am presupposing the traditional view held unchallenged for eighteen centuries that Paul wrote the Epistle to the Ephesians. For an extensive discussion on this topic see C. E. Arnold, 'Ephesians, Letter to the', in *Dictionary of Paul and His Letters*, edited by Gerald F. Hawthorne and Ralph P. Martin (Downers Grove, Illinios: IVP, 1993), 240–42.

116   Ronald Y. K. Fung, *The Epistle to the Galatians*, NICNT (Grand Rapids, MI: Eerdmans, 1988), 175.

117   Graham Hill, *Salt, Light, and a City: Introducing Missional Ecclesiology* (USA: Wipf & Stock Publishers, 2012), 222.

118   A. Johnston, *Missionary Writing and the Empire 1800–1860* (Cambridge UK: Cambridge University Press, 2003), 13. 'In the British Empire, particularly in what is historically known as the "second" era of British imperialism

(approximately 1784–1867), missionary activity was frequently involved with the initial steps of imperial expansion. A heightened sense of religiosity in Britain at this time ensured that Christianisation was seen as a crucial part of the colonialisng and civilising projects of the eighteenth century .....'

119 Of course, as any historian will acknowledge, there were many complex political and social factors at work in addition. However, during the 1800s, the perceived task and methodologies implemented by Christian mission societies were systematically inseparable from the Empires' policy of 'Europeanisation' and 'colonialism' of the new world. As M. E. Page notes, Christianity and colonialism became interdependently interrelated on a global scale. 'Of all religions, Christianity has been most associated with colonialism because several of its forms (Catholicism and Protestantism) were the religions of the European powers, engaged in colonial enterprise on a global scale'. See P. M. Sonnenburg, *Colonialism: An International, Social, Cultural, and Political Encyclopaedia*, Volume 1 (ABC-CLIO Books, 2003), 496.

120 William Carey, *An Enquiry into the Obligations of Christians to use Means for the Conversion of the Heathens* (Pantianos Classics, 1792 reprint 2016), 29.

121 Lausanne Movement, *Story of Lausanne,* http://www.lausanne.org/about-the-lausanne-movement.

122 Lausanne Movement, *Lausanne Covenant,* http://www.lausanne.org/content/covenant/lausanne-covenant.

123 K. Hester, *Free Will Baptists and the Priesthood of All Believers* (Nashville: The Historical Commission of the National Association of Free Will Baptists, 2010), 5.

124 DeYmaz and Li, *Ethnic Blends*, 50.

Chapter 10

125 Rodney Woo discovered this at Wilcrest Baptist Church. While the church had been declining in membership a renewed vision focusing on multiethnicity saw several newcomers enter the church. Unfortunately, Wilcrest struggled to retain these new comers. After conducting several exit interviews, Rodney identified especially from those of African-American origins that the most obvious reason was that they had not done enough to bridge the ethnic gaps. One of the key gaps was still in leadership. See Woo, *Color*, 202.

ENDNOTES

126 DeYmaz, *Building*, 71; see chapter six of this book for another helpful discussion of this topic.

127 Woo, *Color*, 201.

128 C. Peter Wagner, *Leading Your Church to Growth: The Secret of Pastor/People Partnership in Dynamic Church Growth* (California: Regal Books, 1984), 88–89.

129 Ibid.

130 Robert Greenleaf (1904–1990), a former AT&T executive, originally coined the term in a 1970 essay titled 'The Servant as Leader', which in 1977 would be published into a book. Robert K. Greenleaf, *Servant Leadership: A Journey Into the Nature of Legitimate Power and Greatness* (New Jersey: Paulist Press, 1977; reprint 2002). So pervasive is this idea of servanthood in the leadership function that modern secular authors on leadership have taken the servant model and applied it to corporate businesses. See for instance Ken Blanchard and Phil Hodges, *The Servant Leader: Transforming Your Heart, Head, Hands and Habits* (Nashville: Thomas Nelson, 2003).

131 Greenleaf, *Servant*, 27.

132 Graham Hill, *Servantship: Sixteen Servants in the Four Movements of Radical Servantship* (Eugene, OR: Wipf and Stock, 2013), 2–3.

133 Aubrey Malphurs, *Building Leaders: Blueprints for Developing Leadership at Every Level of Your Church* (Grand Rapids, MI: Baker Books, 2004), 10.

134 Robert Russell, 'A Practical Theology of Servant Leadership', *School of Leadership Studies*, (2003): 1; 1–9. Contextually, the servant leader Isaiah spoke of has been identified as the nation of Israel who serve God, a faithful remnant who serves God even in the difficulties of the exile and ultimately the Messiah who would epitomize all this and more as a suffering servant. See Stanley M. Horton, *Isaiah: A Logion Press Commentary* (Springfield, Mo.: Logion Press, 2000), 480.

135 H. W. Beyer, 'Diakonos' in G. Kittel, ed., and G. W. Bromiley, ed. and trans., *Theological Dictionary of the New Testament*, vol. II (Grand Rapids, MI: Eerdmans, 1964), 88. Also William H. Willimon, *Calling and Character: Virtues of the Ordained Life* (Nashville: Abingdon, 2000), 17. The terms found in Act 6 refers to 'waiting on tables'. See David G. Peterson, *The Acts of the Apostles*, Pillar NTC (Nottingham: Apollos, 2009), 233. Rom 1:1, 15:16; Phil 1:1; Titus 1:1; Jas 1:1; 2 Pet 1:1; Jude 1:1.

136 The prophetic interpretation of the identity of the suffering servant is a controversial subject. For a discussion on the different identifications see Howard Young, 'Rediscovering Servant Leadership' *Enrichment Journal*, http://enrichmentjournal.ag.org/200202/200202_032_serv_leader.cfm. What is unmistakeable however is the underlying servantship theme and the over 35 NT allusions to chapter 53. Darrell Jackson, 'For the Son of Man Did Not Come to Serve, but to Lead,' in Hill, *Servantship*, 16.

137 John F. MacArthur, *Called to Lead: 26 Leadership Lessons from the Life of the Apostle Paul* (Nashville: Thomas Nelson, 2010), v.

138 I have adopted this quote from the writings of John Maxwell. However, it is not clear who the original source is. Some have ascribed it to Teddy Roosevelt. See John C. Maxwell, *Developing the Leader Within You* (Nashville: Thomas Nelson Books, 1993), 7.

139 Ronnie Floyd, *10 Things Every Minister Needs to Know* (Green Forest, AR: New Leaf Press, 2006), 19.

140 Oswald Chambers, *My Upmost for His Highest* (Grand Rapids: MI, Discovery House Publishing, 1992), 17.

141 Dave Earley and Ben Gutierrez, Ministry *Is ...: How to Serve Jesus with Passion and Confidence* (Nashville: B&H Publishing Group, 2010), 78.

142 Frost and Hirsch, *Shaping*, 54.

143 Grae McWhirter, 'Seeing Mission as Organising Function' in Hill, *Servantship*, 112–13.

144 Ibid., 113.

145 McWhirter, *Seeing Mission*, 113.

146 Frost and Hirsch, *Shaping*, 85; David Bosch, 'Transforming Mission: Paradigm Shifts' in *Theology of Mission* (Maryknoll, NY: Orbis, 1991), 89: 'The Christian faith is intrinsically incarnational ... Therefore, unless the church chooses to remain a foreign entity ... it will always enter into a context in which it happens to find itself'.

147 Alan J. Roxburgh, *Missional: Joining God in the Neighbourhood* (Grand Rapids: Baker Books, 2011), 171.

148 Graham Hill, Salt, *Light and a City: Introducing Missional Ecclesiology* (Eugene, Oregon: Wif & Stock, 2012), 271.

149 Woo, *Color*, 209.

150 Walter L. Liefeld, *1 & 2 Timothy and Titus* NIVAC (Grand Rapids: Zondervan, 1999), 118.

151 R. T. France, *The Gospel of Matthew*, NICNT (Grand Rapids: Eerdmans, 2007), 353.

152 This is the traditional and belief about the Gospel's authorship. For a further discussion see Craig S. Keener, *The Gospel of Matthew: A Socio-Rhetorical Commentary* (Grand Rapids: Eerdmans, 2009), 38–40.

153 Gordon D. Fee, *Paul's Letter to the Philippians*, NICNT (Grand Rapids: Eerdmans, 1995), 406–7.

ENDNOTES

154 Mark E. McBeth, *The Distributed Leadership Toolbox: Essential Practices for Successful Schools* (California: Corwin Press, 2008), 36. See also Rinehart, *Upside Down*, 29.

155 DeYmaz, *Building*, 70–80.

156 Bennie E. Goodwin, *The Effective Leader: A Basic Guide to Christian Leadership* (Illinios: IVP, 1971), 8.

157 J. Oswald Sanders, cited in Mathew Philip, *You Can Lead Effectively!* (USA: Xulon Press, 2008), 73.

158 For an introduction to various leadership styles see Ted W. Engstrom, *The Making of a Christian Leader* (Grand Rapids: Zondervan, 1977), 67–82.

Appendix 1

159 Donald A. McGavran, *Understanding Church Growth* (Grand Rapids, MI: Eerdmans, 1970), 73.

160 Jurgen Moltmann, *The Open Church: Invitation to a Messianic Lifestyle* (London: SCM, 1978), 27–36.

161 For a brief discussion about the life, influences and legacy of McGavran see George G. Hunter, 'The Legacy of Donald A. McGavran', *International Bulletin of Missionary Research* 16 no. 4 (1992):158–62.

162 McGavran, *Understanding*, 81.

163 Ibid., x.

164 Frost and Hirsch, *Shaping*, 73.

165 For an easy to read and fairly brief discussion of the topic see Mark DeYmaz, *HUP: Should Pastors Accept or Reject the HUP?* eBook available via Mosaix Global Network, http://www.mosaix.info/resources/hup.

166 Extracts from McGavran's response letter dated April 24, 1978. Letter cited in Gary McIntosh, *The Life and Ministry of Donald A. McGavran: A Short Overview*, McIntosh Church Growth Network, http://churchgrowthnetwork.com/free-resources/2010/05/25/the-life-and-ministry-%09of-donald-a-mcgavran.

167 Frost and Hirsch, *Shaping*, 73.

168 Moltmann, *Open Church*, 30–31.

169 DeYmaz, *HUP*, 11.

Appendix 2

170   Everett M. Rodgers, *Diffusion of Innovations* (New York: Free Press, 2003).

171   Helen Richmond and Myong Duk Yang, *Crossing Borders Shaping Faith: Ministry and Identity in Multicultural Australia* (Sydney: National Assembly of the Uniting Church in Australia, 2006), 316.

Appendix 4

172   For a good overview of the rhetorical flow of Paul's argument see Gordon D. Fee *The First Epistle to the Corinthians* NICNT (Grand Rapids, MI: Eerdmans, 1987), 357.

Appendix 5

173   Emerson, *Divided by Faith*, 141.

174   Woo, *Color*, 181.

175   Ibid., 180–81.

176   Ibid., 187.

177   Kathy Black, *Culturally Conscious Worship* (St Louis: Chalice, 2000), 69.

178   Michael Emerson with Rodney Woo, *People of the Dream: Multiracial Congregations in the United States* (Princeton: Princeton University Press, 2006), 136–37.

179   Black, *Culturally*, 80.

180   Woo, *Color*, 189.

181   George Yancey, *One Body One Spirit: Principles of Successful Multiracial Churches* (Downers Grove: IVP, 2003), 81.

182   DeYmaz, *Building*, 59.

Appendix 6

183   Ben Witherington III, *The Acts of the Apostles: A Socio-rhetorical Commentary* (Grand Rapids, MI: Eerdmans, 1998), 392.

184   DeYmaz, *Building*, 23.

185   Peterson, *Acts*, 374.

186   F. S. Spencer, *Acts* (Sheffield: Sheffield Academic, 1997), 137.

Appendix 8

187 For some excellent scholarly discussion on the role of women in the early church see Richard Bauckham, *Gospel Women: Studies of the Named Women in the Gospels* (Grand Rapids, MI: Eerdmans, 2002).

ACKNOWLEDGMENTS

Undertaking the writing of this book has been a long-term project for me. For over ten years, I have had a desire to tell the story of Parkside Church, but felt the timing wasn't right. I also needed the right people to help.

I am thankful to Jason Jeremiah for helping me put my ideas and thoughts into writing.

I would like to express my gratitude to Darrell Jackson for reading the manuscript and for his insightful suggestions. Thank you also for writing the foreword.

Thank you to Vivian Grice for reading the manuscript and offering valuable comments.

I am grateful to Morling Press for enabling me to publish this book.

I am deeply indebted to my church family at Parkside Church for their love, support and encouragement. They are the inspiration behind and reason for this book.

Nobody has been more important to me in the writing of this book than the members of my family. I want to express my sincere gratitude to my loving and supportive wife, Savi. Thank you for standing beside me over the years in the pursuit of a vision to grow a healthy multiethnic church. I am also very thankful to our children, Sherina, Jason and Vivian, for their constant support and unending inspiration.

ABOUT THE AUTHOR

Mathew Kuruvilla has been the Senior Pastor of Parkside Baptist Church in Sydney, Australia for over 30 years. Parkside Church is a diverse community, with people from over 60 different nations making it their home. Mathew has several years' experience in cross-cultural ministry including time on board *Logos* and ministering among various communities in India. Mathew is a graduate of Morling College and has been pastoring churches in Australia since 1983. He is married to Savi and they have two adult children: a daughter, Sherina, and a son, Jason, married to Vivian.